MURDER DOG
THE COVERS VOLUME ONE

FOUNDED BY Black Bone Dog
EDITED BY Black Dog Bone & Paul Stewart

PUBLISHED BY

Murder Dog The Covers Vol. 1
2015 © Murder Dog / Rain Face Eye
Over The Edge Publishing

ISBN: 978-1-944082-12-3 (paperback); 978-1-944082-09-3 (hardcover)
Cover & Design by Michael Ziobrowski for X Is The Weapon

All rights reserved. No part of this book may be reproduced or transmitted in any form or by any means, electronic or mechanical, including photocopying, recording, or by information storage and retrieval systems, without the written permission of the publisher, except by a reviewer who may quote brief passages in a review. Printed in the United States of America.

overtheedgebooks.com

CONTENTS
THANK YOU 4
INTRODUCTION 5
THE COVERS 9

ARTIST	PHOTOGRAPHER
50 Cent	*Marcus Hanschen*
Al Kapone	*Marcus Hanschen*
Plies	*Eric Johnson*
Strange Music	*Black Dog Bone*
2 Chainz	*John Ricard*
Z-Ro	*Marcus Hanschen*
50 Cents	*Marcus Hanschen*
Yung joc	*Eric Johnson*
August Alsina	*John Ricard*
Beanie Sigel	*Marcus Hanschen*
BG	*Rachel Holland*
Big Boi	*Eric Johnson*
Big Tymers	*Marcus Hanschen*
Big Tymers	*Marcus Hanschen*
Brother Lynch Hung	*Black Dog Bone*
Brother Lynch Hung	*Marcus Hanschen*
Bow Wow	*Eric Johnson*
Cali Swag District	*Eric Johnson*
Chamillionaire	*Lionel Deluy*
Chingy	*Marcus Hanschen*
C-Murder	*Marcus Hanschen*
C-Murder	*Marcus Hanschen*
D4L	*Eric Johnson*
Dark Lotus	*Eric Johnson*
David Banner	*Barry Underhill*
David Banner	*Marcus Hanschen*
Darkroom Familia	*Marcus Hanschen*
Dawn Raid	*Barry Underhill*
Dayton Family	*Jade Scott Santos*
DAZ	*Barry Underhill*
D J Khaled	*Marcus Hanschen*
Drama	*Marcus Hanschen*
Dungeon Family	*Marcus Hanschen*
E-40	*Marcus Hanschen*
Eight Ball & MJG	*Marcus Hanschen*
Federation	*Marcus Hanschen*
G-Unit	*Marcus Hanschen*
Red café/French Montana	*John Ricard*
Game	*Lionel Deluy*
Game	*Lionel Deluy*
Game	*Lionel Deluy*
Game	*Lionel Deluy*
Freddie Gibbs	*Black Dog Bone*
Grind Family	*Marcus Hanschen*
Ice Cube	*Marcus Hanschen*
Ice Cube	*Marcus Hanschen*
Insane Clown Posse	*Marcus Hanschen*
Insane Clown Posse	*Johnny Buzzerio*
Hot Boys	*Marcus Hanschen*
Jacka	*Marcus Hanschen*
Jackson MS	*Marcus Hanschen*
JT	*Marcus Hanschen*
Juvenile	*Marcus Hanschen*
Juvenile	*Marcus Hanschen*
JT	*Marcus Hanschen*
Juvenile	*Marcus Hanschen*
Sick Wid It	*Marcus Hanschen*
Sick Wid It	*Marcus Hanschen*
Keak Da Sneak	*Marcus Hanschen*
Keak Da Sneak	*Marcus Hanschen*
Keak Da Sneak	*Marcus Hanschen*
Keak Da Sneak	*Marcus Hanschen*
KRS One	*Marcus Hanschen*
Lil Wayne	*Lionel Deluy*
Lil John	*Eric Johnson*
Lil John	*Marcus Hanschen*
Mac Dre	*Black Dog Bone*
Mac Dre	*Black Dog Bone*
Mac Mall	*Marcus Hanschen*
Krizz Kaliko	*Marcus Hanschen*
Kotton Mouthkings	*Lionel Deluy*
Machine Gun Kelly	*Eric Johnson*
Master P	*Marcus Hanschen*
May Day	*Marcus Hanschen*
MC Eight	*Marcus Hanschen*
Messy Marv	*Marcus Hanschen*
Mistah Fab	*Marcus Hanschen*
Mobb Deep	*Marcus Hanschen*
Montana	*Black Dog Bone*
Nappy Roots	*Marcus Hanschen*
Natas	*Jade Scott Santos*
Nelly	*Marcus Hanschen*
Omaha	*Black Dog Bone*
Out Kast	*Marcus Hanschen*
Pastor Troy	*Marcus Hanschen*
Paul Wall	*Eric Johnson*
Project Pat	*Eric Johnson*
Psychopathic	*EWolf*
Pusha	*T Nabil*
Raekwon	*Marcus Hanschen*
Rick Ross	*Eric Johnson*
San Quinn	*Marcus Hanschen*
Scarface	*Jack Thompson*
Slaugter House	*John Ricard*
The Wyld	
Soulja Slim	*Marcus Hanschen*
Soulja Boy	*Lionel Deluy*
Talib Kweli	*Marcus Hanschen*
Tech9	*Black Dog Bone*
Tech9	*Marcus Hanschen*
Tech9	*Marcus Hanschen*
Thizz	*Marcus Hanschen*
Three 6 Mafia	*Black Dog Bone*
Too Short	*Marcus Hanschen*
TI	*Lionel Deluy*
TI	*Eric Johnson*
Town Thizz	*Shemp of Doctor Graphics*
C-Murder	*Marcus Hanschen*
Turf Talk	*Marcus Hanschen*
Tyga	*John Ricard*
UGK	*Deron Neblett*
Seattle	*Black Dog Bone*
Webbie	*Marcus Hanschen*
Westside Connection	*Marcus Hanschen*
Wale	*Lionel Deluy*
Warren G	*Marcus Hanschen*
Xzibit	*Marcus Hanschen*
Xzibit	*Marcus Hanschen*
YG	*John Ricard*
Young JeEzy	*Eric Johnson*
Yuckmouth	*Marcus Hanschen*
Yuckmouth	*Barry Underhill*

THANK YOU

FOR MARY DOWNS.
THIS BOOK AND ALL THE MURDER DOG BOOKS ARE FOR YOU. WITHOUT YOU THERE WOULD BE NO MURDER DOG. THANK YOU FOR EVERYTHING.

TO ALL THE PHOTOGRAPHERS WHO TOOK PHOTO'S FOR MURDER DOG, THANK YOU SO MUCH.
I LOVE YOU.

MARCUS HANSCHEN, ROY YOSHIOKA, ERIC JOHNSON, LIONEL DELUY, BARRY UNDERHILL, JOHN RICARD, DERON NEBLETT, KEBA KONTE, MATT SONZALA, DAVE KATZ, JASON LAMOTTE, BRIAN BARTHOLOMEW, STEVE ROBERTS, GEZUS ZAIRE.
SCOTT BEJDA, DAVID FRIEDMAN, DAIKA BRAY, BRAD SADLER, MATT SONZALA, ALLEN GORDON, J.DOGG, LOU NUT, FLAGGS, GEZUS ZAIRE, COURTNEY OMEGA, TED WILLIAMS, CHARLIE BRAXTON, RICK THORNE, BRIAN BARTHOLOMEW, DAVE KATZ, GREG DAVENPORT, NANDA PABA, RICHARD D, AL KAPONE, NIKI GATEWOOD, ADELL HENDERSON, KEITA JONES, PAUL ARNOLD, SOREN BAKER, X-RAIDED, DOLLAR BILL KELVIN, ROOT DOCTOR, CHIEF HYDRO, RICHARD HENDERSON, JAVON ADAMS, MJ RASOOL, BEN LEWIS, DOUBLE E, JD HILL, RAY RAY AKA RED BIRD, GARWYNE JONES, MADUMA SALIKA, KEVIN SHORT, WENDY DAY, JIM DOWNS, RENE MORALES, BRIAN LASSITER. PK, DIRTY J, V TOWN.

ALSO THANK YOU TO MATT SONZALA, ANDREW NOSNITSKY, PAUL STEWART, FOR HELPING TO MAKE MURDER DOG BOOKS HAPPEN.

INTRO

OTE Books - What can you tell us about the process of picking the cover photos at Murder Dog?

Black Dog Bone – When we pick the cover we go for the feeling more than anything that inner spirit, not the outside. We always tell the artist look right at the camera. So when you look at a Murder Dog cover you connect with the person. You know the eyes connect you to your heart. It's that connection that we always look for. When we work on a cover for Murder Dog, we go through like one hundred to two hundred photos, and then we would scan or go through the best twenty to thirty photos. Then we would narrow it down to about to about ten to twelve photos, then we would make covers from all of them, we always have about eight or nine covers that never made it, but are equally good that would be a book on it's own, the covers that never made it to the final cover. After that we would send it to our printer, then they would send the color keys back then we would make covers and put them up on the wall. Then we will ask everyone what their favorite is – but it's always this one cover we all pick, the cover that's going to happen just comes up – and we all know it's going to be the one. Doing the covers for Murder Dog takes as much time and work as doing the whole magazine. Some happen fast, some take awhile. It's easy if we have good photos but sometimes the photos are not as good as we want them to be, Doing covers is so much fun: I love making covers.

OTE Books- Did that process change as the magazine grew?

Black Dog Bone – No it never really changed. We always did it the same way but the look of the cover kept changing, we had many different styles – we would get into one style and keep doing it for awhile, then we would get on to another style, it always kept changing. At the start I did all the photos, I did the covers and the photos that we used on the layout pages. As we started getting big it was too much work for me, I just couldn't do it, I used to always be on a plane going to Memphis or Houston or Kansas or Atlanta or up north to Seattle or Portland, or down south to San Diego or LA. I mean I was always traveling. The last cover I did was for 36 Mafia. The first few years it was a big format news print magazine, it was like 14 by 11, real big, the covers were also black and white. That 36 mafia cover was the first cover we did the regular magazine format, it was the first full color glossy issue, after that issue I stopped doing covers.
I had met Marcus from Paris. He used to do all the covers for Paris's label G Funk. He had done Conscious Daughters and many other covers.. The first cover we had done with a studio set up was at Marcus's studio. He had a studio south of Market in San Francisco, that's where we did most of the early covers, the first cover Marcus did was C-Bo. He became our main photographer in the early days he did all the covers, he did 50 Cent, Snoop, Ice Cube, Nelly, Wu Tang Clan, E40, to many to name them all, he did hundred's, and he is still here with us. He still works for Murder Dog.
I remember with the C BO cover he had just got out of jail. We were all waiting for him to come out, C BO is my all time favorite rapper! I love all his earlier albums that Mike Mosley produced with AWOL records. C- Bo's album had that dark mysterious grimy feeling- and it was real gangsta – I still love those albums and I always play them, I love C BO he is the best. He is one of those people.
Different covers opened different doors for us. With the 36 Mafia cover we went to a full glossy magazine, it was the first one we did the regular magazine size – with that magazine we got major distribution, we were in all the chain stores everywhere, when we did 36 mafia they were totally unknown outside of Memphis, they hadn't even got signed yet, but they were so good I knew they were going to be real big, basically the sound the south has is the Memphis sound, that 36 Mafia, Al Kapone, Skinny Pimp, Player Fly –doing was the sound that became

the Atlanta Crunk sound that became big with Lil John. It was that Memphis gangster walk beat everyone was influenced by that sound from Master P and all the No Limit artists to Cash Money records. The 36 Mafia cover really opened many doors for us it was at this time Master P who had been living in Richmond CA and had moved his No Limit records to the south.

OTE Books - Do you regret any covers?

Black Dog Bone – We never regret anything we did with Murder Dog. It's that we always did what we wanted, we really don't care what everybody else was doing or saying, we didn't have to try to please any one, not the record labels, not the industry- Whatever we felt, what ever we want to do, we did it, we still do it that way.

OTE Books- How much did what was on the cover effect the sales of each issue?

Black Dog Bone – Certain covers at the beginning effected sales, but once people got to know Murder Dog, whoever we had on the cover didn't matter, people just bought it for the name they always knew they were always going to get what other magazines didn't have – more then major artists we did underground artists, I mean we always had artists other people never had, like DJ Screw, E Shaun, Insane Clown Posse, Tech 9, I mean it's so many.

The Cover that made Murder Dog what it became was the cover we did with Master P. IT was called No Limit Explosion it came out at the time Master P had just got signed to Priority. I took that photo in LA outside at Barbara's apartment. Barbara was the one who did publicity for No Limit records and we knew her real well. Me and Barbara and Master P were at her apartment, it was almost dark, I took the photos just outside her apartment then we got Pen and Pixel to do the cover- it was big that cover really blew up Murder Dog – It was a real nice cover it was still on the 14 by 11 size magazine – we were still doing that, the cover was our first color cover. It really put Murder Dog on another level – At this time Master P was just breaking through and everyone wanted to know about him and we were the only people to have a big story on him and No Limit records and have him on the cover.

The success of Murder Dog has a lot to do with Master P. I love Master P and C- Murder – I love C- Murder he is the best. Master P really supported us – He used to always have like six to eight full-page ads. When people saw he was advertising with Murder Dog and he was the biggest thing to ever happen everyone started advertising with us, especially the major labels – they all started coming with Murder Dog our sales went way up – we were printing truck loads – it was big – we couldn't keep up. It was such a demand – then everyone started advertising with us before it was mostly Bay area and Southern ads like Suave House and Rap a lot – then the major labels all opened their doors – next thing was Cash Money we were the first ever magazine to do a story on Cash Money – they were not even signed!! But they were real big in New Orleans area me and a lot of Murder Dog people went to Juvenile's record release party – which they had it in a record store – we met everyone, Little Wayne was just a little kid like 12 or 13 years old – no tattoos or nothing – Baby and Ron and Mannie Fresh, Hot Boys everyone was there – then they also started really supporting Murder Dog – they also started to put six to eight ads in Murder Dog – Baby and Ron are just real cool people – we love Cash Money – I have met so many good people doing Murder Dog – so many and I love them all. So many beautiful things I remember what an amazing time it was,

We were so big in the South - the Deep South loved Murder Dog –I was spending more time in Memphis and Nashville and Baton Rouge then. I would take six to eight people from Murder Dog we would get a hotel their for weeks six to eight people all in two rooms – it was insane they were the happiest times I remember..

I spent a lot of time in Memphis with Al Kapone – also there was a person who worked for Murder Dog called

Garwin from Memphis – I used to stay at his house and J Dawg from Select- O -Hits was there too and we would always go to Visit No Limit records in Baton Rouge. We spent a lot of time in Nashville too. I had a person who worked for us called MJ Razzol – He was a radio DJ who played underground music – He also did work with Pistol. Sadly he died from an accident working at a factory.

OTE Books - Who was on the first cover?

Black Dog Bone – The first cover of Murder Dog that we did was Young "D" Boyz. The cover was a picture of Squatos from Young "D" Boyz and on the back cover we had Bugg Bop AKA Khadhaffi, who was also from Young "D" Boyz. We were living in the Southside of Vallejo, it was Porter Street. We first lived in the Hillside, and then we moved to Southside—that's where Murder Dog started. Porter Street, the Southside , that was the street where everything was going on. All night, all day, something was happening. There were cops out there all the time. And there was chickens and roosters and misquotes.

When we did the first cover we had big names in that issue like Wu Tang Clan, Fugees, Coolio, Onyx, but we decided to put Young "D" Boyz on the cover. They were from the Southside and they had just put out their CD on River T Records; the label was also from the Southside. Young "D" Boyz' album is just so amazing! It really captures the feeling of South Vallejo/Porter Street, like hot summer days, that desolate dry mysterious feeling. It's like the times of the Blues in the rural South. The atmosphere they created in that record is so real, so dark. It's a very melancholy record. There is some kind of desperation in that record. Khayree (Young Black Brotha) and John Dillinger did most of the production. It's one of my all time favorite records. It's out of print, but if you can find it get it. The Young "D" Boyz were realer than real and I so happy we had them on the cover. I feel like them being in the cover is what made Murder dog what it was. I've seen people selling the first issue of Murder Dog on EBay for like 200 dollars and up. Even us, we only have a very few copies.

OTE Books - Were a lot of artists upset when they didn't get the cover?

Black Dog Bone – Just a few were. But we pretty much have done almost all the artists on our covers, from the biggest to the most underground to the most hardest. All the southern artists, Midwest artists, we've done a lot of East Coast artists too. We've done Biggie Smalls; we did Wu Tang Clan, DMX, Nas, KRS-One, Busta Rhymes, Jay Z, Mob Deep, Talib Kweli. Really we have done everyone. We've done all of the West Coast artists, all of them, and everyone in the Bay too. And the Midwest too. Then we've even done cover stories on Dancehall artists like Sizzla, Junior Kelly, Ward 21. We did a whole issue on Garage music from UK—we had So Solid Crew on that cover. We did a special issue on Go Go music from DC with Chuck Brown on that cover. We did K'Naan from Somalia. We did a cover for Dawn Raid that's a label from New Zealand, we had Savage and Monsta Ganjah on the cover. We have done a lot of white rappers too, from Yelawolf to Kottonmouth Kings, Swollen Members, Slain and Machine Gun Kelly. Then all the artists who do Horrorcore have been on Murder Dog covers, like Insane Clown Posse, Brotha Lynch Hung, Esham, Natas, Twiztid, Kung Fu Vampire. It's so many! We've really done it all. And for most of the artists it was their first cover. Some of these artists are legendary but no other magazines had given them a cover—artists like Tech N9ne, E-40, Jacka, Soulja Slim, Three-6 Mafia, Messy Marv, Mac Dre, JT Money, C- Bo, David Banner, Rick Ross, Master P, Cash Money…legends!

OTE Books - Were you proud to put artists on the covers that would never be on the covers of other Rap magazines?

Black Dog Bone – We were. We always wanted to put artists who were real, who were original. We really didn't care if they were real big or if they were signed to a major label or even if they had a big following or if they had sold any records. There are a lot of artists that are doing things that no one else is doing, very creative, very original, very real. We kept putting artists like that. We wanted the world to know there was this artist who was doing amazing music but never got signed or made it big. Like DJ Screw or Esham or Mac Dre, Dayton Family, UGK. Freddie Gibbs, Grind Family, Insane Clown Posse, Jacka, Yukmouth. A cover I really wanted to do that never happened was M.I.A. When she was first getting big here I was in Sri Lanka. I was living in the rain forest, I was really out of it so we missed out on M.I.A. But we did do a cover for one of her artist Rye Rye.

OTE Books– What artist was the happiest or most shocked they were getting a cover?

Black Dog Bone – Most artists were happy to get the Murder Dog cover. Especially the East Coast artists, so many of them wanted the Murder Dog cover. They all knew how big we were in all the prisons. And also they knew the most hardcore fans, everyone in the hood, read Murder Dog. We had a big underground following. It was like, "OK we have all the other magazines, but we want to be in the Murder Dog!" It kind of showed, I'm in this hardcore underground magazine and they give me respect as an artist." When we'd do a cover it was always a big event. Sometimes artists would come like two-three cars full of their people, or all the artists signed to their label, all the girls, the guns…I mean everything! They were big all-day events. I have so many stories, I mean too many to write now. That would be another book, for sure.

When we'd go to shoot the cover we'd take like 300 to 500 shots, with different outfits, different concepts. We have thousands of photos of every rapper. We have a whole storage with steel cabinets full of prints and negatives. Later on we even started filming cover shoots, but that only happened recently. To me what's so exciting is when I would go to a rapper's house or a studio or a radio station to see Murder Dog covers blown up on the wall.

Just a few weeks ago Rick Ross' people wanted the cover jpeg of the Rick Ross cover we did. That was his first cover. It was just around the time he got signed. We also used to make large posters of all our covers and blast them all over in every city. We would put hundreds of them wall to wall; they were all over!

Another thing that made our covers so special and so good was all the photographers we used. Like I said, Marcus Hanschen was the first and main photographer who did most of our covers. He is amazing. One of the best people I met. I just love Marcus. Then we had Eric Johnson, who is also really good. He is from ATL. Eric Johnson a wonderful person, another one of those special people. Then we worked with Barry Underhill, another cool person, really nice. Then later we worked with Lionel Deluy, another great photographer. He did some amazing covers for Murder Dog. He did all the Game covers. The one image we are using on the cover of the book, he did that. Later we started using John Ricard a lot. He's from New York, real good, real good. I love working with John Ricard , even Matt Sonzala did covers. What can I say about Matt Sonzala, there is only a few people like him. v a very few good people like Matt. All the photographers we ever used were real good. But more than that, they were the coolest people, really good people. And that made a big difference. To me that was everything. That's what made Murder Dog what it is, working with people like that, just down to earth, simple, real people.

THE COVERS

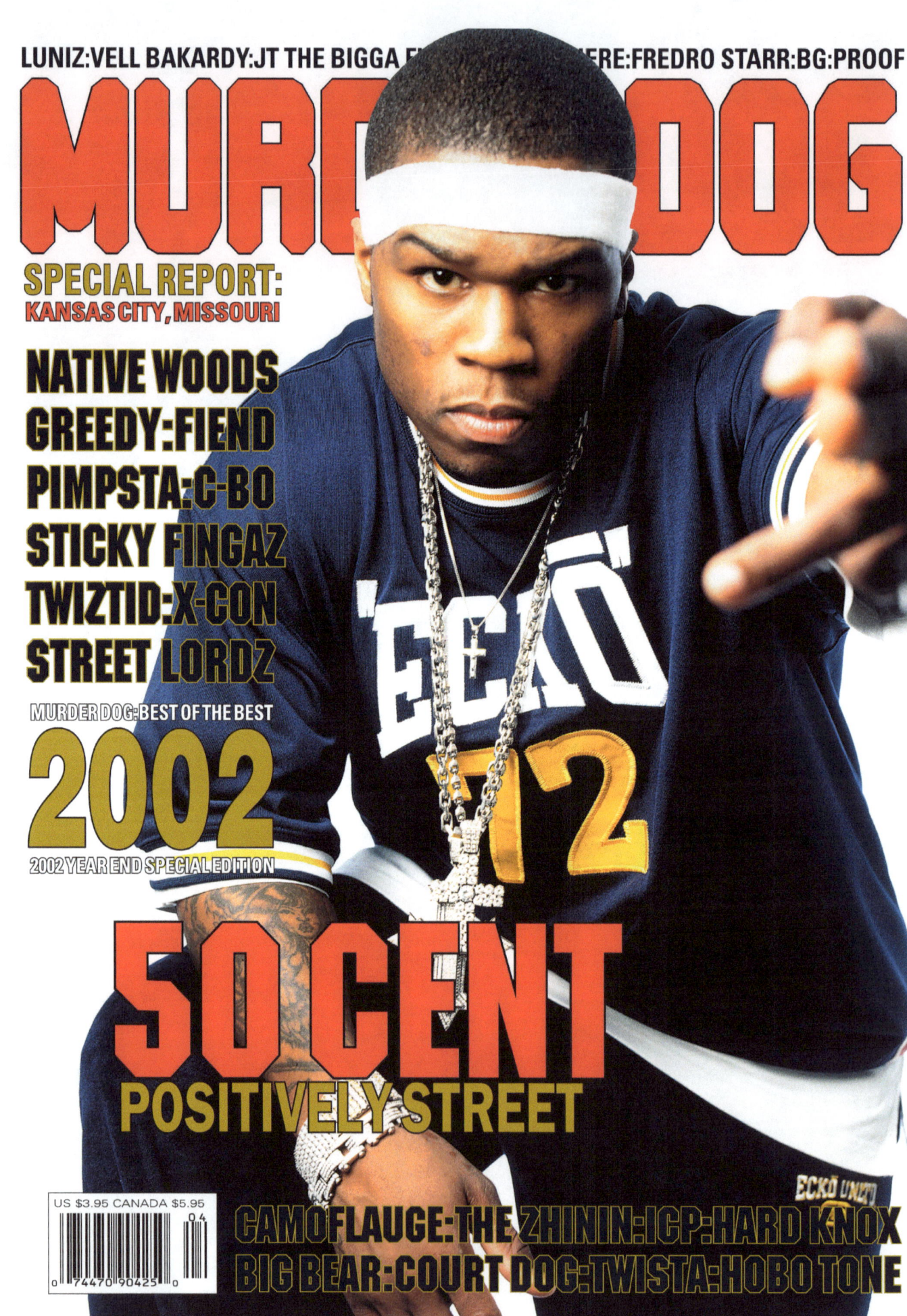

SERVIN THA WORLD CLICK:BIG TYMERS:KORN:ICE T:CHILEE POWDAH:E-40:RAEKWON

MURDER DOG

SPECIAL FEATURE
DETROIT UNDERGROUND

MURDER DOG BEST OF THE BEST

99

1999 YEAR END SPECIAL EDITION

SUPER CRUNK
AL KAPONE

US $2.95 CANADA $3.95

PASTOR TROY:PLAYA FLY:YOUNG DROOP:GANGSTA BLAC
INSANE CLOWN POSSE:SKAMBINO MOB:TWIZTID:NATAS

MIKE JONES:SLIM THUG:C-MURDER: THE GAME:GUCCI MANE

MURDER DOG

SPECIAL REPORT:
AUGUSTA:GEORGIA

PLUS:
CELLY CEL:BLADE
BOYZ N DA HOOD
EMPACT STRONG
PIMPZILLA:1504
DOUBLE CROSSA
SLIM-BO:C-BALL
T-MAC:MILLI MAE
MEMPHIS BLEEK

BEEFIN
Z-RO:DON'T START NOTHIN

US $3.95 CANADA $5.95

PASTOR TROY:JAYO FELONY:C.O. THA! BAD BLACK
CIRCLE BOYZ:BLOUNT AVE:AL KAPONE:YOUNG GUNZ

MIKE JONES:HUSTLAM... ...TSIDE BOYZ:BENZINO

MU... ...OG

SPECIAL REPO...
MAC DRE & THIZZ NA...

PLUS:
LUDACRIS:UGK
DAVID BANNER
GAME:DIRTBAG
DSR:HUSALAH
MONEY WATERS
MANNIE FRESH
ROBLO:T-ROCK
TOCKA:RYDAH

50 CENT
GETTIN CRUCIAL

US $3.95 CANADA $5.95

EVIL PIMP:MAC MALL:YOUNG JEEZY:FAT KILLAHZ
KING TERRA:PAUL WALL:BLOODRAW:CUBAN LINK

GANGSTA BOO:EASTSIDAZ:LIL JON & THE EASTSIDE BOYZ:PASTOR TROY:KURUPT:BAD AZZ

MURDER DOG

SPECIAL REPORT:
ATLANTA,GA/CHICAGO,IL

PLUS:
BACKBONE
TECH N9NE
TURK:COG
DEEP SOUTH
SNYPAZ:AZ
COURT-DOG
QUEEN PEN

BEANIE SIGEL
POINT BLANK

GHETTO MAFIA:YOUNG DROOP:CRUCIAL CONFLICT
MOSSIE:KOKANE:TRAXTER:KURUPT:CAMOFLAUGE

US $3.95 CANADA $5.95

LUNIZ:50 CENT:JT THE BIGGA FIGGA:RICK ROSS:DAMN-SHAME:DOC:RIC JILLA:PROOF

MURDER DOG

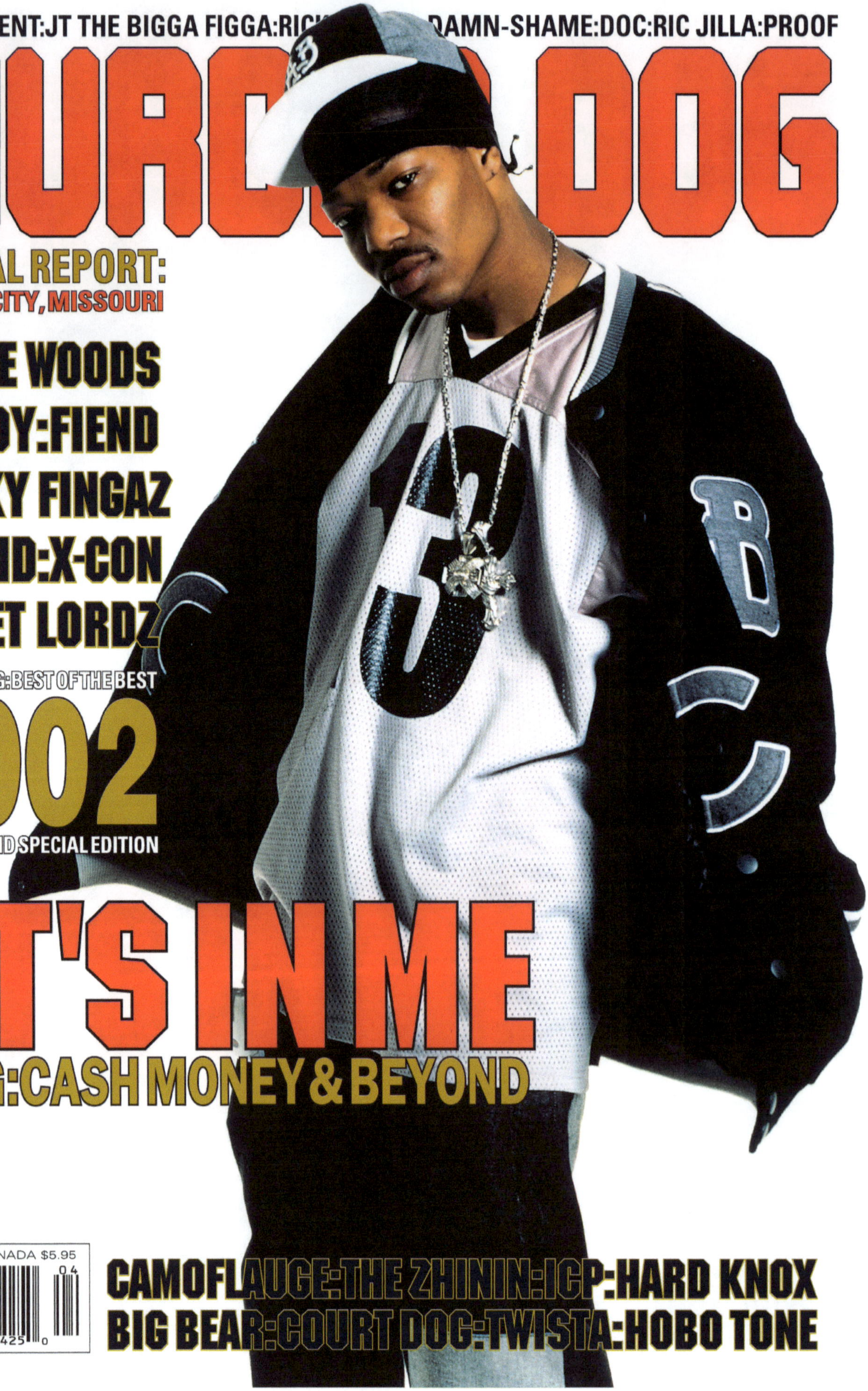

SPECIAL REPORT:
KANSAS CITY, MISSOURI

NATIVE WOODS
GREEDY:FIEND
STICKY FINGAZ
TWIZTID:X-CON
STREET LORDZ

MURDER DOG:BEST OF THE BEST
2002
2002 YEAR END SPECIAL EDITION

IT'S IN ME
BG:CASH MONEY & BEYOND

US $3.95 CANADA $5.95

CAMOFLAUGE:THE ZHININ:ICP:HARD KNOX
BIG BEAR:COURT DOG:TWISTA:HOBO TONE

BIG BOI:THE GAME:ALI SW... DISTRICT:MESSY MARV:... ...A:JUVENILE

MURDER DOG

PLUS:
BIZARRE:TECH N9NE
TWIZTID:BOONDOX
COOL NUTZ:BLACK C
SWAG:MANIAC LOK
POLITICAL ASSASSIN
KOSHIR:REZ HEADZ
KING GORDY:LIL RIC
MIA:PROJECT BORN
E-40:FIRST DEGREE

BOW WOW
FLIGHT VERTICAL

$4.95US

CAPONE-N-NOREAGA:ANYBODY KILLA:SLUM VILLAGE
KOTTONMOUTH KINGS:AMPICHINO:YOUNG BOSSI

MAC DRE:MISTAH FAB:BONE THUGS-N-HARMONY:MIKE JONES:INSANE CLOWN POSSE

MURDER DOG

SPECIAL REPORT:
NEW BAY AREA PRODUCERS

PLUS:
PROPHET POSSE
ICE T:TURF TALK
TRAX-A-MILLION
ROBLO:DROOP-E
HAJI:MAC MALL
PROJECT BORN
E-40:TECH N9NE
KEAK DA SNEAK

CYCLONE
CHAMILLIONAIRE

$3.95US $5.95CAN

BEEDA WEEDA:JOHNNY CASH:AMPLIVE:COOLNUTZ
REDMAN:AWAX:THE PACK:YOUNG BUCK:BIG RICH

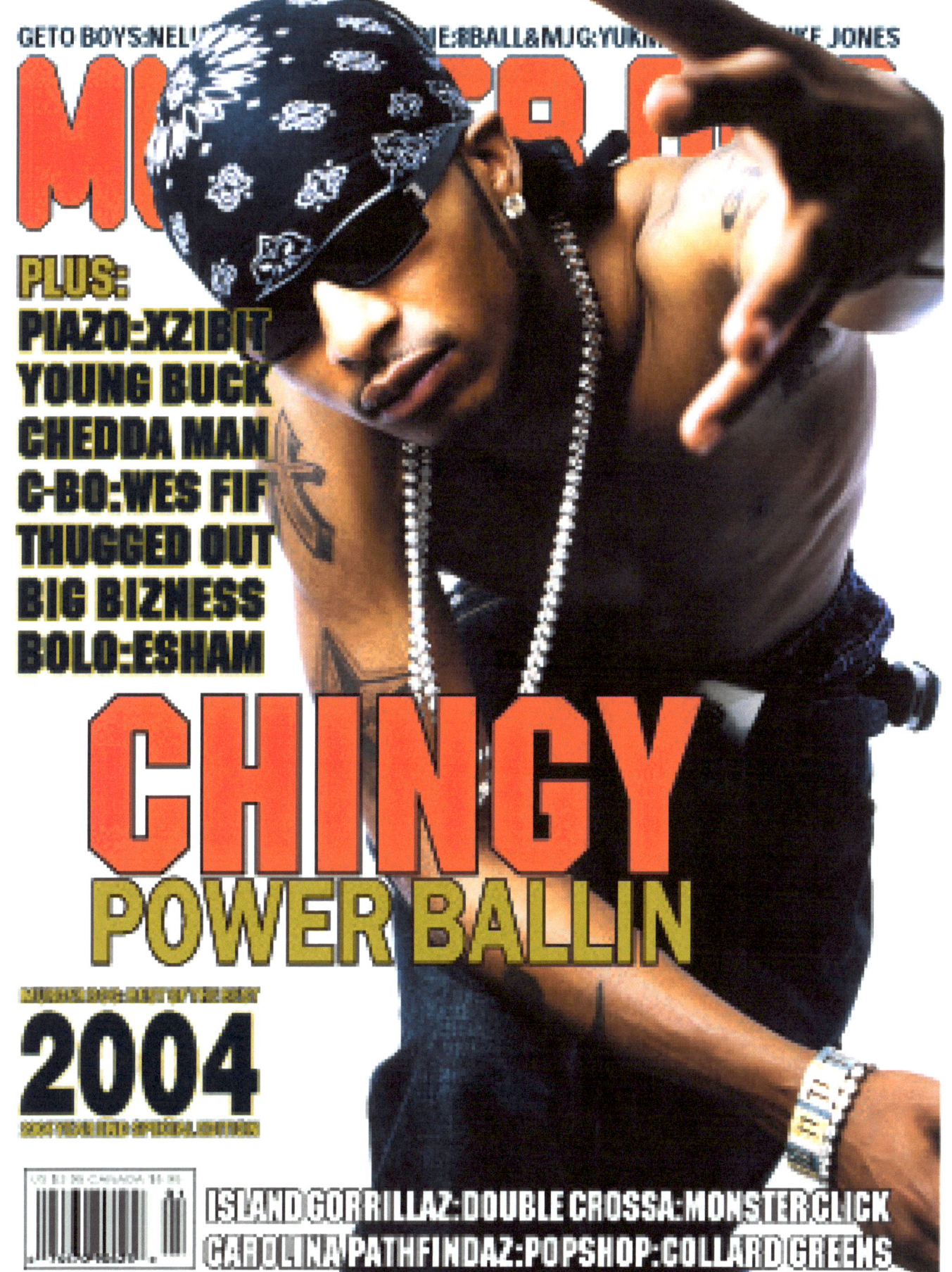

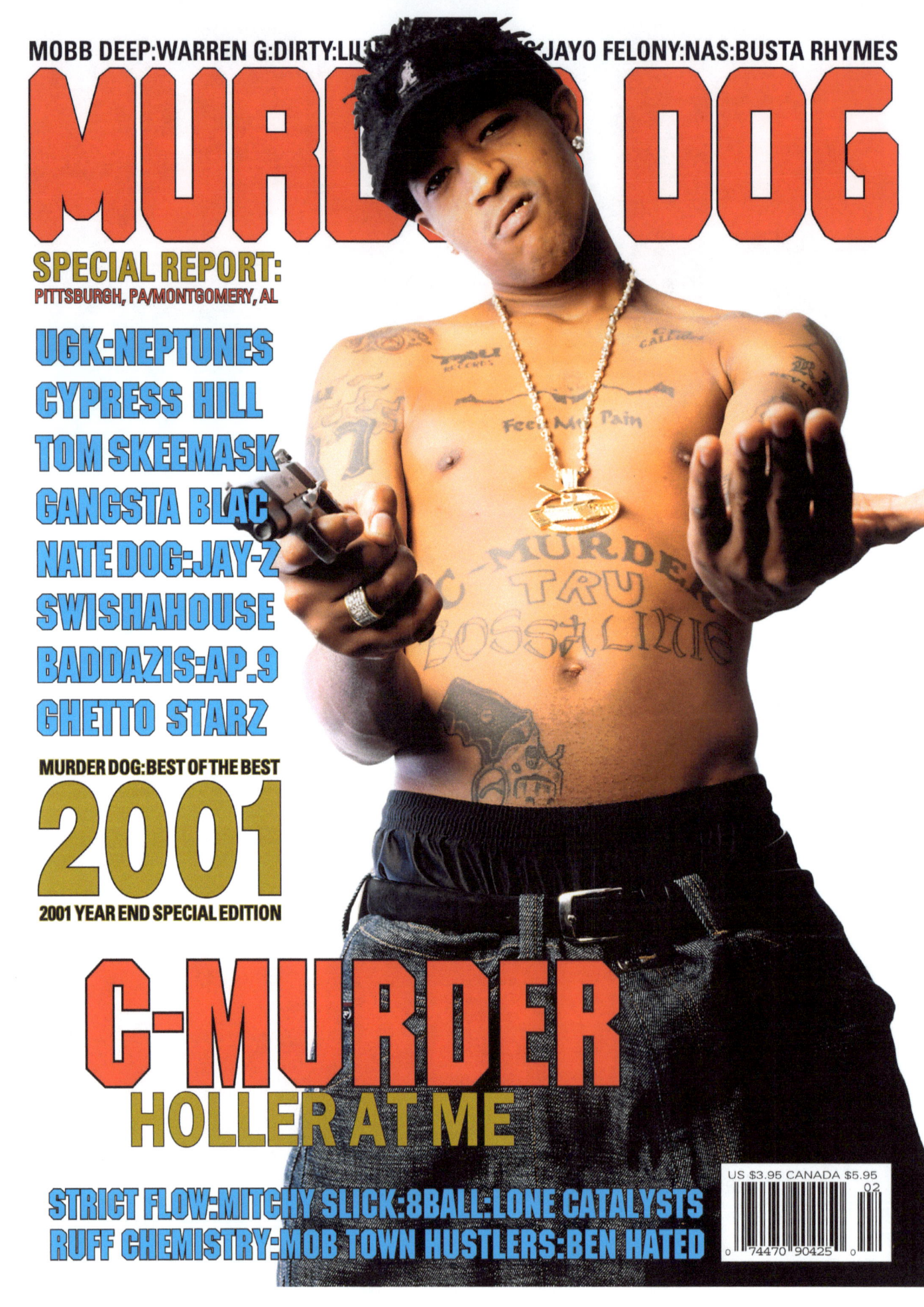

THE GAME:MIKE JONES:HOO... ...LAWZ:SLIM THUG:BOYZ IN D...

MURDER D...

SPECIAL REPORT:
AUGUSTA:GEORGIA

PLUS:
CELLY CEL:BLADE
PIMPZILLA:1504
EMPACT STRONG
Z-RO:GUCCI MANE
DOUBLE CROSSA
SLIM-BO:C-BALL
T-MAC:MILLI MAE
MEMPHIS BLEEK

C-MURDER
REFUSE TO LOSE

US $3.95 CANADA $5.95

PASTOR TROY:JAYO FELONY:C.O. THA! BAD BLACK
CIRCLE BOYZ:BLOUNT AVE:AL KAPONE:YOUNG GUNZ

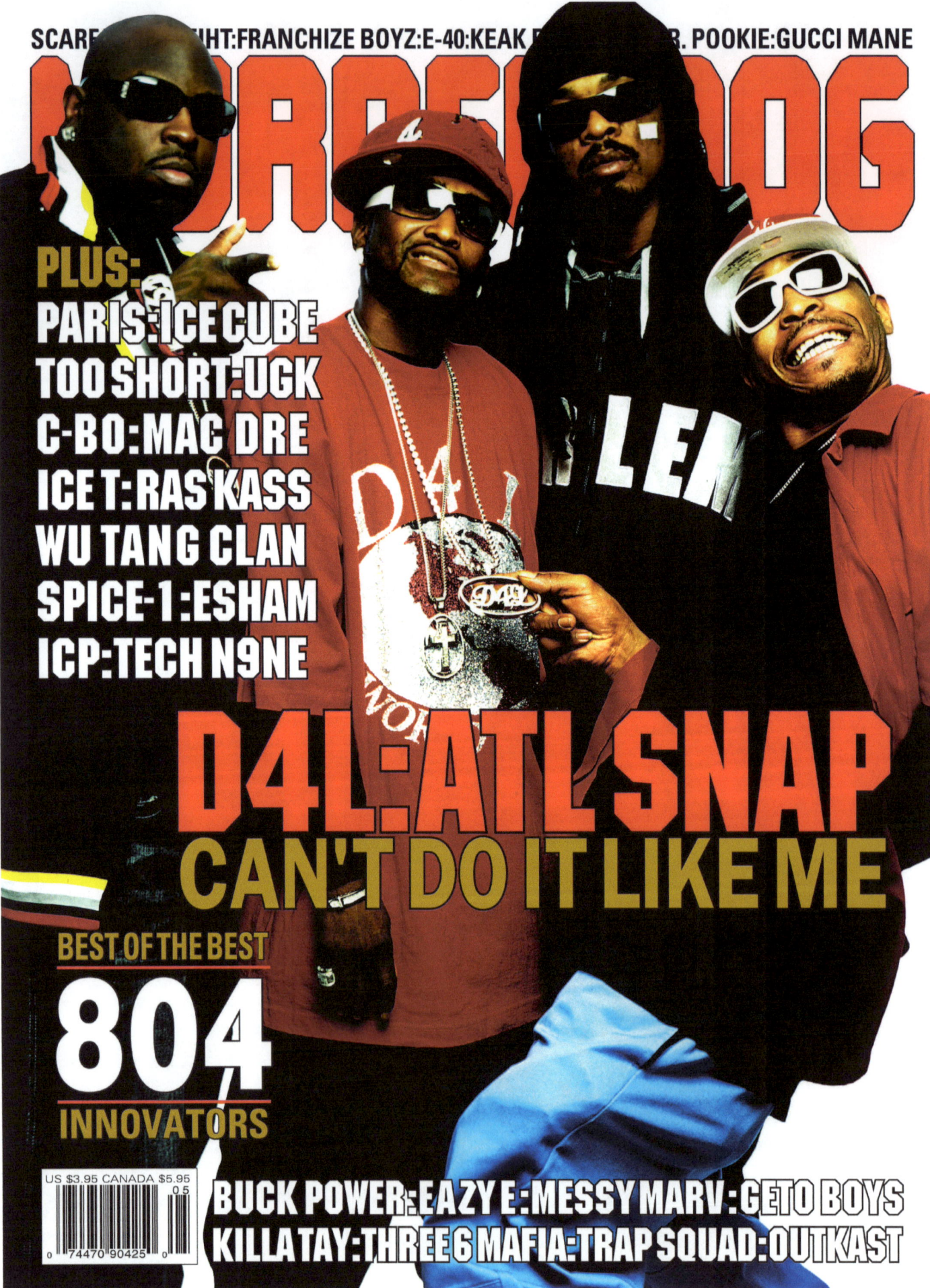

KEAK DA SNEAK:G-UNIT:DIRTBALL:BOONDOX:BIG RICH:PLIES:YUKMOUTH:TECH N9NE

MURDER DOG

MURDER DOG SPECIAL: SRI LANKAN RAP

PLUS:
KRIZZ KALICO
40 CAL:G-UNIT
BROOKLYN ZU
DIZZEE RASCAL
CARLO SAUCE
ELEPHANT MAN
KILLER MIKE

MURDER DOG CELEBRATING
15 YEARS
MURDER DOG CELEBRATING

DARK LOTUS
EVOKING THE EVIL

$3.95US $5.95CAN

SUE COE:LI-YOUNG LEE:ZHOU BROTHERS:DAVID WOLFE
BATHIYA & SANTHUSH:IRAJ:CHINTHY:BONE KILLA

PAUL WALL:M... ...NG TWINS:TONY YAYO:YOUNG JEEZY:WEBBIE

PLUS:
BIZARRE:TURK
MIKE JONES:AZ
BLACK SMOKE
MITCHY SLICK
DIRTY:CAPONE
LSR:CZARNOK
PLAYAZ CIRCLE
BIG MIKE:KLC

DAVID BANNER
SPILLIN BLOOD

US $3.95 CANADA $5.95

DAYTON FAMILY:YOUNG BLEED:CRIMINAL MANNE
NOCTURNAL RAGE:YO GOTTI:C.O.THA! BAD BLACK

TRICK DADDY:JT MONEY:DMX:JT THE BIGGA FIGGA:BG:JAY-Z:SOUTH PARK MEXICAN

MURDER DOG

SPECIAL REPORT:
SAN DIEGO UNDERGROUND

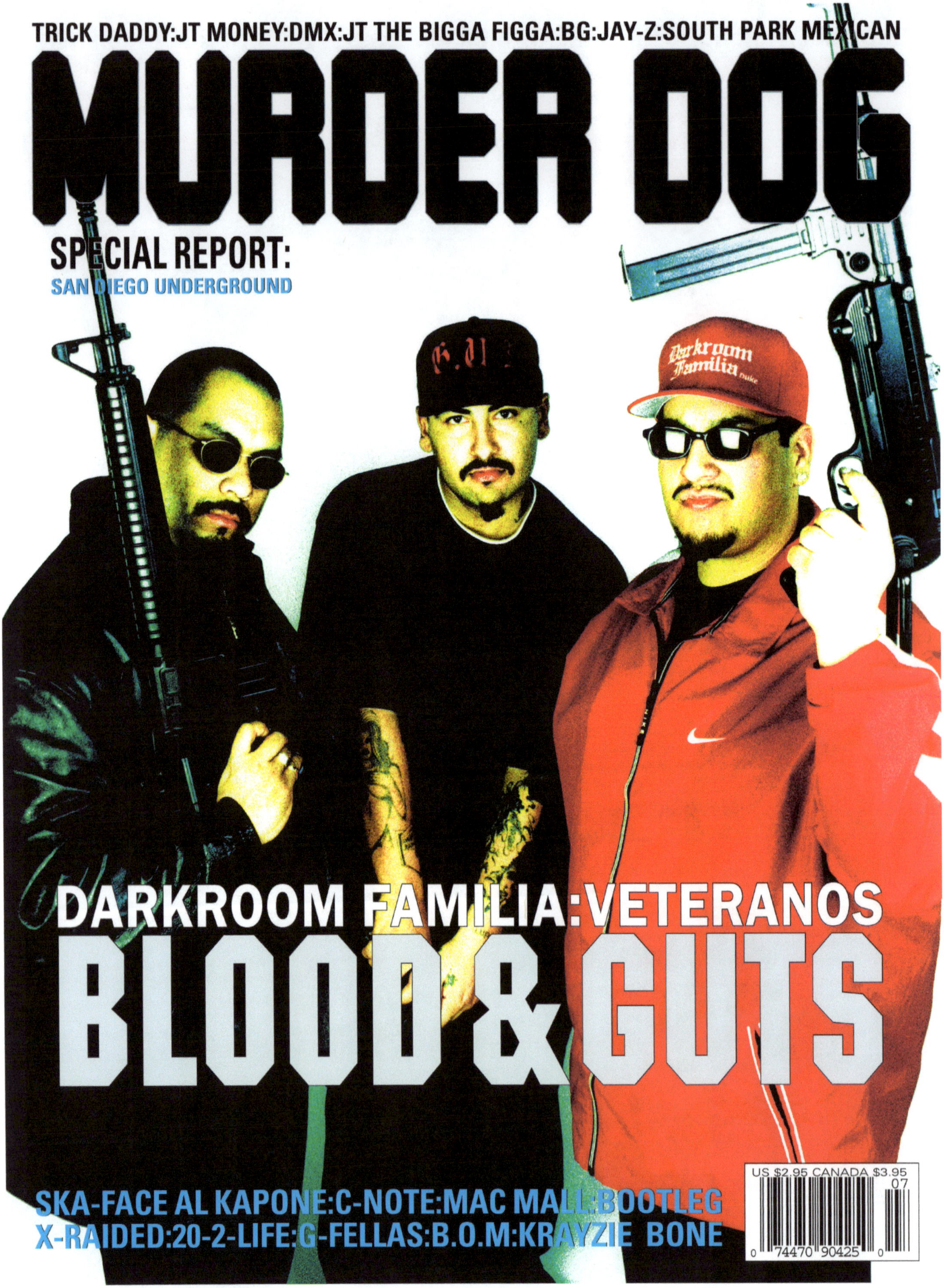

DARKROOM FAMILIA:VETERANOS
BLOOD & GUTS

SKA-FACE AL KAPONE:C-NOTE:MAC MALL:BOOTLEG
X-RAIDED:20-2-LIFE:G-FELLAS:B.O.M:KRAYZIE BONE

US $2.95 CANADA $3.95

GANGSTA BOO:EASTSIDAZ:PASTOR TROY:BEANIE SIGEL:TURK:QU... AZZ

MURDER DOG

PLUS:
BACKBONE
TECH N9NE
TURK:COG
DEEP SOUTH
SNYPAZ:AZ

DAYTON FAMILY
FLINT:MICHIGAN

GHETTO MAFIA:YOUNG DROOP:CRUCIAL CONFLICT
MOSSIE:KOKANE:TRAXTER:KURUPT:CAMOFLAUGE

US $3.95 CANADA $5.95

THE GAME:LUDACRIS:KLC:CALI ... THOD MAN

MURDER DOG

PLUS:
TRAX-A-MILLION
DEM HOODSTARZ
TURF TALK:C-BO
BOONDOX:HI-TEK
KLC:CRIME SEEN
X-CLAN:OUTKAST
AK9:YUKMOUTH
POTZEE:SCRAPAZ
SHAWNNA:JUICE

DAZ GLOBAL

US $3.95 CANADA $5.95

TRIPLE DARKNESS:BEEDA WEEDA:MITCHY SLICK
MASTAMIND:BIG RICH:MEGABUCKS:THIZZ LATIN

MURDER DOG

murderdogcollectorsissue

MURDER DOG COLLECTOR'S ISSUE

> I'm just happy to make music for the people. I make music for the people in the streets, that's what I do and I ain't never gonna stop doing that. I can relate to everybody in the streets so I make music for them. I'm reppin every hood in the country.

i'm not a lion but a lion's father
d j khaled

X-RAIDED : JAY ROCK : GAME : YOUNG JEEZY : KRIZZ KALIKO
TECH N9NE : LIL WAYNE : YELAWOLF : WAKA FLOCKA FLAME

$4.95US

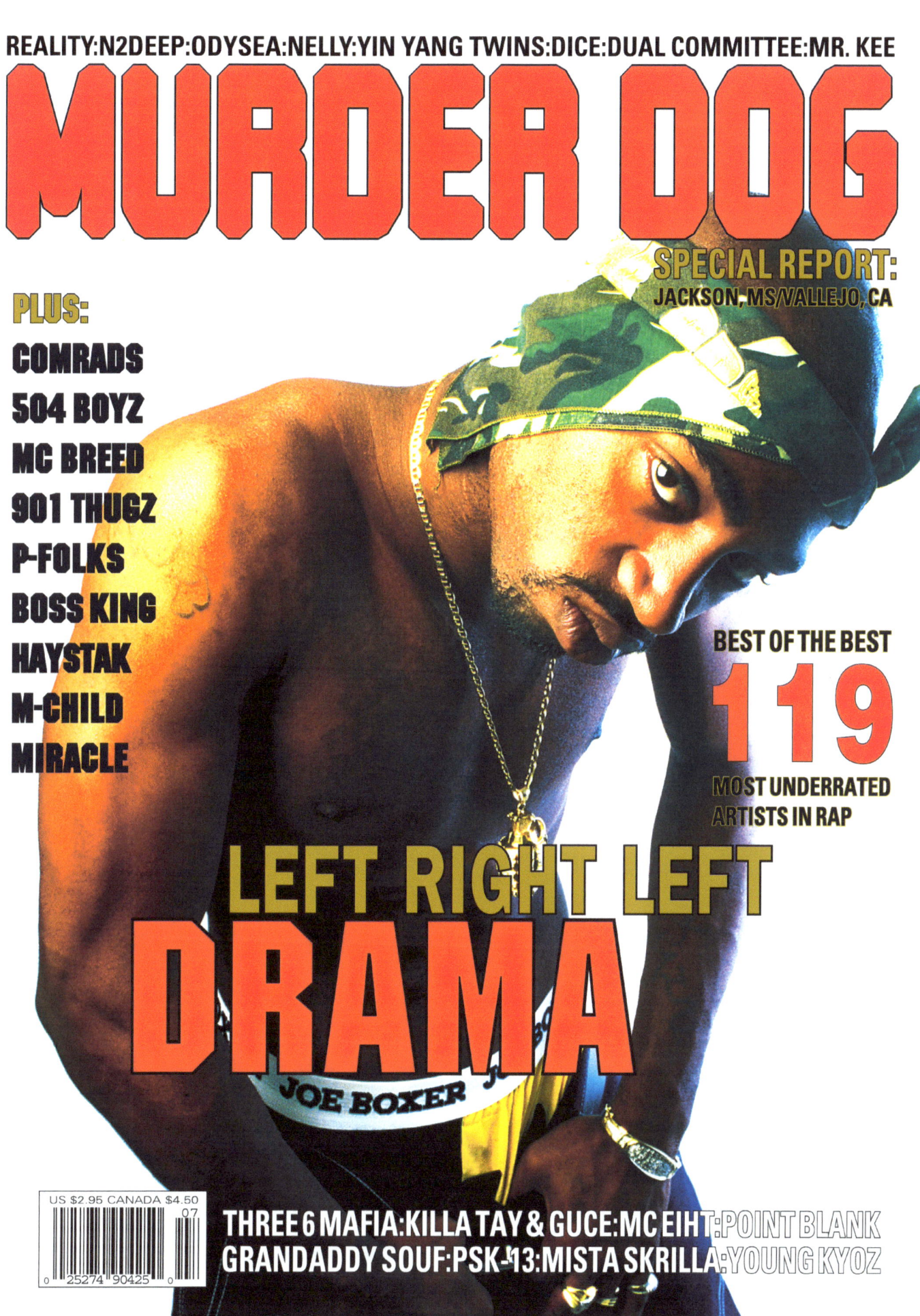

REALITY:N2DEEP:ODYSEA:NELLY:YIN YANG TWINS:DICE:DUAL COMMITTEE:MR. KEE

MURDER DOG

SPECIAL REPORT: JACKSON, MS/VALLEJO, CA

PLUS:
COMRADS
504 BOYZ
MC BREED
901 THUGZ
P-FOLKS
BOSS KING
HAYSTAK
M-CHILD
MIRACLE

BEST OF THE BEST
119
MOST UNDERRATED ARTISTS IN RAP

LEFT RIGHT LEFT
DRAMA

US $2.95 CANADA $4.50

THREE 6 MAFIA:KILLA TAY & GUCE:MC EIHT:POINT BLANK
GRANDADDY SOUF:PSK-13:MISTA SKRILLA:YOUNG KYOZ

MOBB DEEP:LIL FLIP:YOUNG BUCK:MC EIHT:LIL SCRAPPY:EC ILLA:CORMEGA:DO OR DIE

MURDER DOG

PLUS:
KURUPT:LUKE
STREET BOSS
MERC SQUAD
STREET KINGZ
BOSS PIMPS
ICP:POTLUCK
THUG LORDZ

GO DUMB
FEDERATION

TURF TALK:IMMORTAL SOLDIERZ:TERROR SQUAD
BUKSHOT:GOODFELLA:WEST COAST MAFIA:MAC DRE

US $3.95 CANADA $5.95

trench montana
red café
murder
bringing new york hip hop back

These days are special days for the sound of Hip Hop. I can't see anybody sayin it's at a standstill. I see it growing all the time. The artists are grossing a lot of money and they're giving back a lot. I feel good about where Hip Hop is going, and we feel ready to give our contribution.

(L - R): RED CAFÉ AND FRENCH MONTANA

$4.95US

X-RAIDED : BAD LUCC : B-CIDE : DON TRIP : T-NUTTY : PROZAK
TECH N9NE : PROBLEM : SPANK ROCK : MAYDAY : KILO CURT

LUDACRIS:LIL SCRAPPY:DAZ:CALI... :METHOD MAN

MURDERDOG

PLUS:
TRAX-A-MILLION
DEM HOODSTARZ
TURF TALK:C-BO
BOONDOX:HI-TEK
KLC:CRIME SEEN
X-CLAN:OUTKAST
AK9:YUKMOUTH
POTZEE:SCRAPAZ
SHAWNNA:JUICE

GAME
FLIP A COIN

US $3.95 CANADA $5.95

TRIPLE DARKNESS:BEEDA WEEDA:MITCHY SLICK
MASTAMIND:BIG RICH:MEGABUCKS:THIZZ LATIN

ICE CUBE:GUCCI MANE:BUSY SIGNAL:M... :SAN QUINN

MURDER DOG

**SPECIAL FEATURE:
MALIDOMA SOMÈ**

**PLUS:
DAZ:TECH N9NE
WILLIE THE KID
MAINO:J-STALIN
MJG:ACE HOOD
J-DIGGS:ESHAM
THREE 6 MAFIA
DEVIN:HAYSTAK
KUTT CALHOUN**

THE GAME
KILLIN IT AS ALWAYS

BEEDA WEEDA:LEP BOGUS BOYS:SUNNY VALENTINE
SKATTERMAN & SNUG BRIM:IMMORTAL SOLDIERZ

murderdogcollectorsissue

MURDER DOG

MURDER DOG
COLLECTOR'S ISSUE

murder
but what else is love
game

X-RAIDED · JAY ROCK · GAME · YOUNG JEEZY · KRIZZ KALIKO
TECH N9NE · LIL WAYNE · YELAWOLF · WAKA FLOCKA FLAME

$4.95US

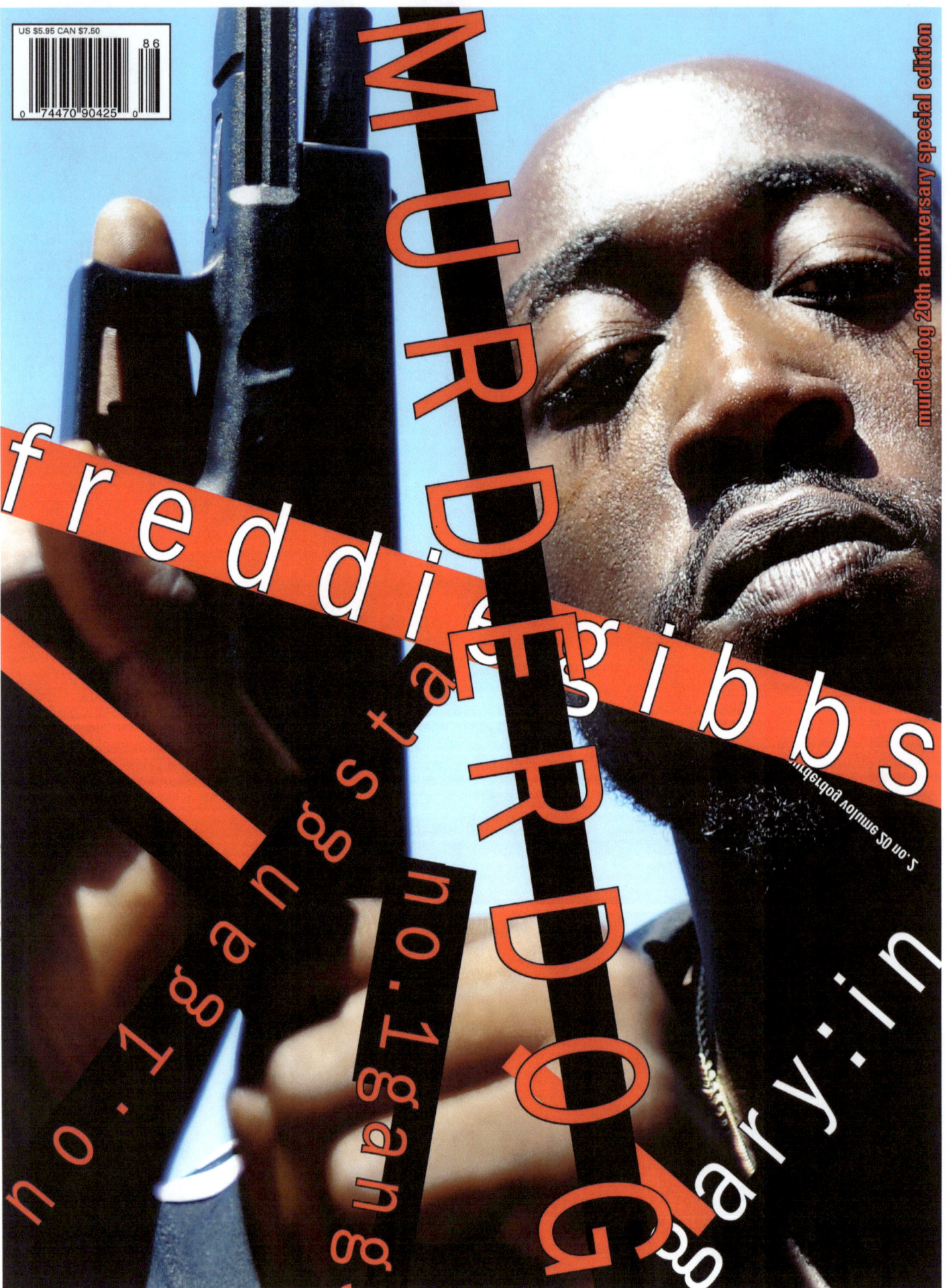

PROJECT PAT:BULLYS WIT FULLYS:TOO SHORT:PROJ... ...ACK

MURDER

PLUS:
- T.I:FEDERATION
- DJ QUIK:FIEND
- FEDX:YUNG JOC
- THE TEAM:C-BO
- DAYTON FAMILY
- UGK:DRU DOWN
- AGALLAH:J-MAC
- SPICE 1:ESHAM
- E-40:BIG HAWK

ICE CUBE
CHROME & PAINT

US $3.95 CANADA $5.95

KILLA KEISE:JUVENILE:TWIZTID:GHOSTFACE KILLAH
LUNI COLEONE:CELLY CEL:LORD JAMAR:THE ZHININ

BONE THUGS-N-HARMONY:DAVID BANNER:MISSY ELLIOTT:LIL JON & THE EASTSIDEBOYZ

MURDER DOG

PLUS:
AP-9:FABOLOUS
TELA:TECH N9NE
PLAYA FLY:HAWK
PRIME FACTORS
ROLLIN' FOX:WC
CLIPSE:MAC DRE
B-LEGIT:ESHAM

DERANGED
INSANE CLOWN POSSE

US $3.95 CANADA $5.95

REESE & BIGALOW:KOOPSTA KNICCA:TOO SHORT
PASTOR TROY:JURASSIC 5:COURT DOG:HOBO TONE

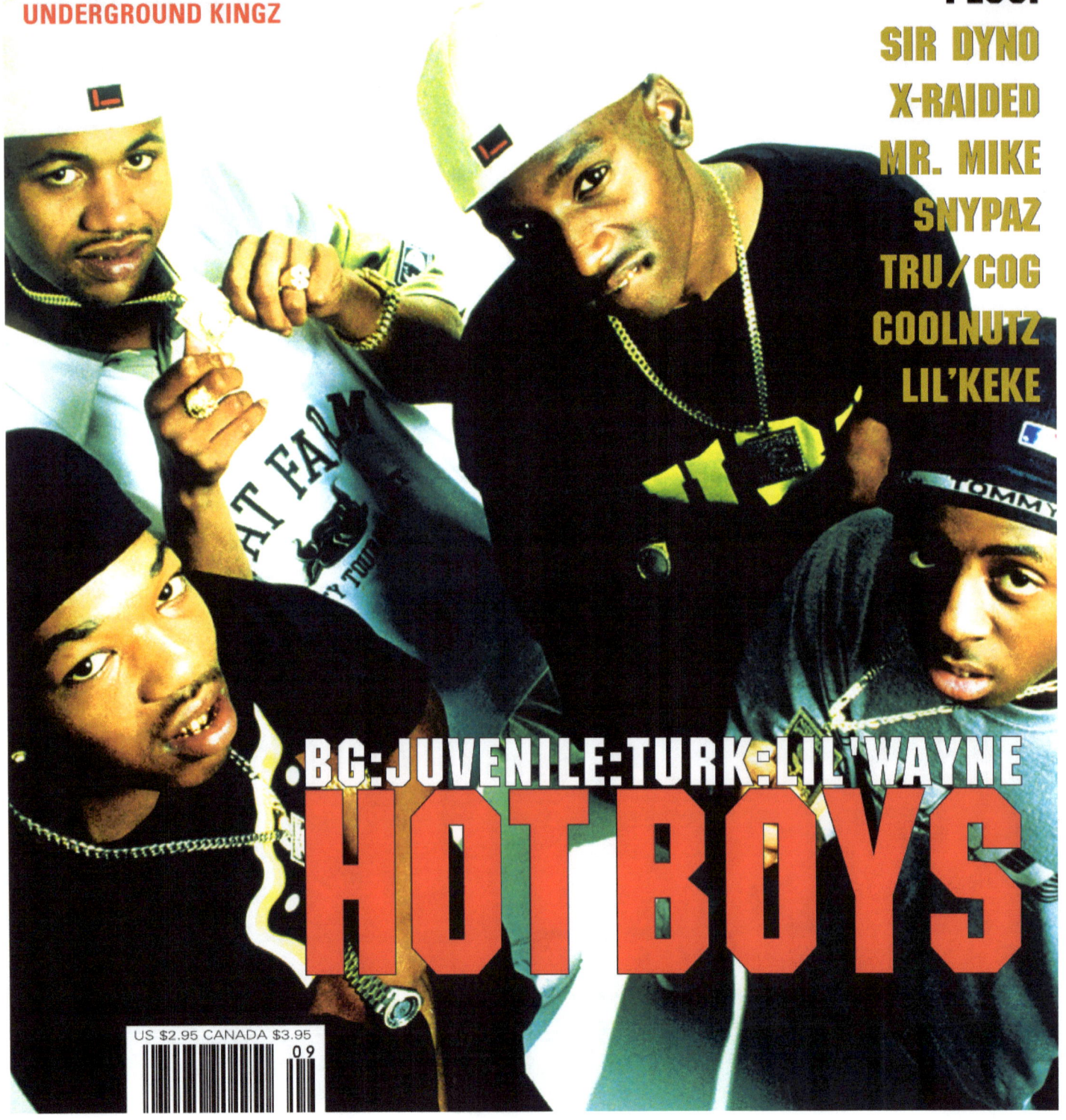

BUSTA RHYMES:TI:LIL WA... ...ARV:UGK:JIM JONES

MURDER DOG

MURDER D...
MC BREED...

PLUS:
ZION I:SAVAGE
PROJECT BORN
STAT QUO:LATE
KEAK DA SNEAK
TECH N9NE:BG
DICE:DJ FRESH
PARIS:X-CLAN
D-LO:SLEEPY D

MURDER DOG: BEST OF THE BEST
2008
2008 YEAR END SPECIAL EDITION

THE JACKA
AFRICAN WARRIOR

$3.95 US $5.95 CAN

DOJA CLIK:12 GAUGE SHOTTIE:OJ DA JUICE MAN
EDDI PROJEX:SLIM THUG:ALFAMEGA:SHADY NATE

KAMIKAZE:DAVID BANNER:MELLO T:US FROM DIRT:LIL JON & THE EASTSIDE BOYZ

MURDER DOG

SPECIAL REPORT:
JACKSON, MISSISSIPPI

BURNIN'
JACKSON:MS

US $3.95 CANADA $5.95

REESE & BIGALOW:KOOPSTA KNICCA:TOO SHORT
PASTOR TROY:JURASSIC 5:COURT DOG:HOBO TONE

TRICK DADDY:DARKROOM FAMILIA:C-NOTE:SOUTH PARK MEXICAN:SKA-FACE AL KAPONE

MURDER DOG

SPECIAL REPORT:
SAN DIEGO UNDERGROUND

-PLUS:

MOB FIGAZ
MC BREED
KACH.22
HELLBORN
G-FELLAS
MAC MALL
SIXX NINE
BOOTLEG
X-RAIDED

JT THE BIGGA FIGGA
SUPER SIZE

BG:KRAYZIE BONE
SNOOP DOGG:DMX

US $2.95 CANADA $3.95
0 74470 90425 0
07

BIG BOI:BOW WOW:THE GAME:CALI SWAG DISTRICT:MESSY MARV:THE GAME

MURDER DOG

**SPECIAL FEATURE:
NATIVE AMERICAN RAP**

PLUS:
BIZARRE:TECH N9NE
TWIZTID:BOONDOX
COOL NUTZ:BLACK C
SWAG:MANIAC LOK
POLITICAL ASSASSIN
KOSHIR:REZ HEADZ
KING GORDY:LIL RIC
MIA:PROJECT BORN
E-40:FIRST DEGREE

JUVENILE
BEAST MODE

CAPONE-N-NOREAGA:ANYBODY KILLA:SLUM VILLAGE
KOTTONMOUTH KINGS:AMPICHINO:YOUNG BOSSI

LUNIZ:50 CENT:BG:RICK ROCK:A-... ...ME:C-BO:RIC JILLA:DOC:PROOF:HITMAN

MURDER DOG

SPECIAL REPORT:
KANSAS CITY, MISSOURI

NATIVE WOODS
GREEDY:FIEND
STICKY FINGAZ
TWIZTID:X-CON
STREET LORDZ

MURDER DOG:BEST OF THE BEST
2002
2002 YEAR END SPECIAL EDITION

RESPECT
JT THE BIGGA FIGGA

US $3.95 CANADA $5.95

CAMOFLAUGE:THE ZHININ:ICP:HARD KNOX
BIG BEAR:COURT DOG:TWISTA:HOBO TONE

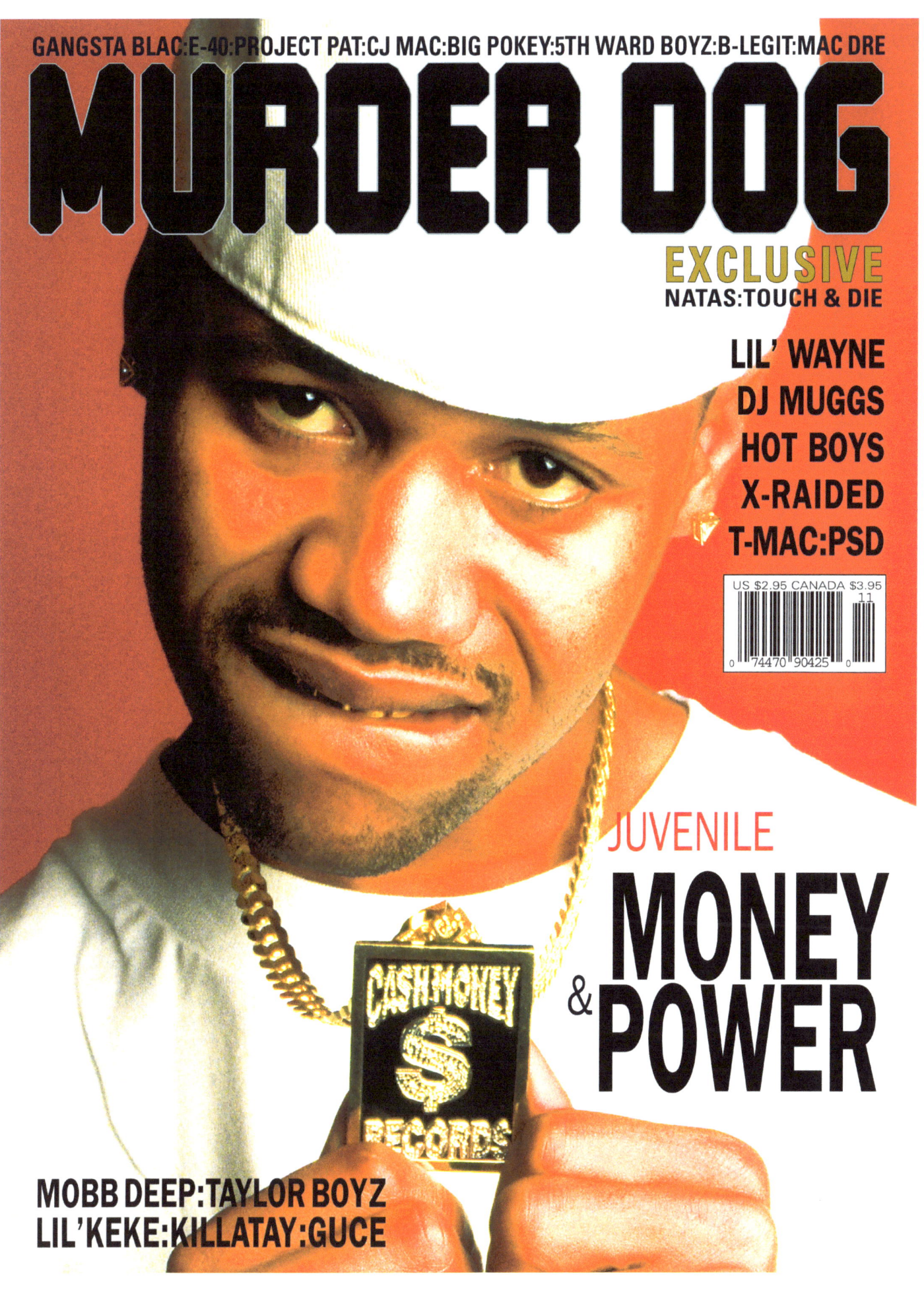

U.S.D.A.:TURF TALK:DROOP E:PASTOR TROY:MUTT DOG:GRANDADDY SOUF:KHAYREE

MURDER DOG

PLUS:
E-40:MAXXIMUM
MAFIOSO:T-HUD
LAROO:RAINMAN
BOYZ-N-DA-HOOD
JD WALKER:HAJI
BLACK C:KALASO
BEBOP:BIG TUCK
YOUNG 'D' BOYZ

SICK WID IT RECORDS
BLOODLINE

BROTHA LYNCH HUNG:RAPPIN 4-TAY:FAT BASTARD
TUM TUM:DANNY TREJO:LIL CHAPPY:MR. DOGTOR

TECH N9NE:KANYE WEST:SQ... DIZZE... ...TSIDERS... ...R P:SAIGON

MURDER DOG

SPECIAL REPORT:
KANSAS CITY:PHILADELPHIA

PLUS:
SPICE 1:TURK
SURVIVALIST
GRIND FAMILY
MC EIHT:GUCE
THUGGED OUT
SKINNY PIMP
LLOYD BANKS
Z-RO:FINESSE

OAKLAND:YES
KEAK DA SNEAK

US $3.95 CANADA $5.95

ELEMENTAL LAW:MIKE JONES:BYRD2BANKS
PAPER DOLL:WESCROOK:HUSTLAMADE BUGZ

DARK LOTUS:G-UNIT: ...KMOUTH:PLIES:TECH N9NE

MURDER DOG

MURDER DOG SPEC...
SRI LANKAN RA...

PLUS:
KRIZZ KALICO
40 CAL:G-UNIT
BROOKLYN ZU
DIZZEE RASCAL
CARLO SAUCE
ELEPHANT MAN
KILLER MIKE

MURDER DOG CELEBRATING
15 YEARS
MURDER DOG CELEBRATING

SPLENDID
KEAK DA SNEAK

SUE COE:LI-YOUNG LEE:ZHOU BROTHERS:DAVID WOLFE
BATHIYA & SANTHUSH:IRAJ:CHINTHY:BONE KILLA

MISTAH FAB:YOUNG JE... ...NE:YOUNGLOODZ

MURDER DOG

PLUS:
KOTTONMOUTH KINGZ
MITCHY SLICK:B-LEGIT
CELLSKI:HOOD STARZ
EVIL PIMP:TURF TALK
FLIP SYDE:YUKMOUTH
DROOP-E:MIKE JONES
CREST CREEPAZ:XZIBIT
MAC DRE:FEDERATION
OUTLAWZ:KILLA KEISE

MURDER DOG: BEST OF THE BEST
2005
2005 YEAR END SPECIAL EDITION

SUPER HYPHY
KEAK DA SNEAK

US $3.95 CANADA $5.95

MESSY MARV:MONY KARLO:WARREN G:SAN QUINN
THREE 6 MAFIA:THE TEAM:RYDAH:YA BOY:MOSSIE

BLACK EYED PEAS:TRICK DADDY:SOULS OF MISCHIEF:EC ILLA:SPICE ONE:GANGSTA DRE

MURDER DOG

SPECIAL REPORT:
WHO'S HOT IN THE BAY!

PLUS:
RBL POSSE
KAM:2PAC
DBA:ICONZ
TALIB KWELI
MAC MALL
JURASSIC 5
YUKMOUTH
SAN QUINN

UNTOLD STORY
KRS ONE

SKINNY PIMP:MESSY MARV:HI-TEK:BIG PUN
DILATED PEOPLES:TOMMY WRIGHT III:SKEE 64

BONE CRUSHER:CASIDDY:KEAK DA SNEAK:SOULJA SLIM:MESSY MA... :ICE MONE

MURDER

PLUS:
- CHINGO BLING
- DAVID BANNER
- CYPRESS HILL
- INDIOTTA:TURK
- THUGGED OUT
- STREET LORDS
- BIG LURCH:BG

BE ATLANTA & CRUNK
LIL JON:LIL SCRAPPY:TRILLVILLE

US $3.95 CANADA $5.95

EASTSIDE CHEDDA BOYZ:C-MURDER:SAN QUINN
PASTOR TROY:COLO-RYDA:STAT QUO:GODXILLA

MIKE J___ ___KA:50 CENT:MAC DRE:NAS:GETO BOYS:MAC___ ___SE

PLUS:
LUDACRIS:UGK
DAVID BANNER
GAME:DIRTBAG
DSR:HUSALAH
MONEY WATERS
MANNIE FRESH
ROBLO:T-ROCK
TOCKA:RYDAH

BUSTIN HEADS
LIL JON & THE EASTSIDE BOYZ

US $3.95 CANADA $5.95

EVIL PIMP:MAC MALL:YOUNG JEEZY:FAT KILLAHZ
KING TERRA:PAUL WALL:BLOODRAW:CUBAN LINK

MISTAH FAB:CHAMILLIONAIRE　　　KE JONES:J-STALIN

MURDER DOG

SPECIAL REPORT:
NEW BAY AREA PRODUCERS

PLUS:
PROPHET POSSE
ICE T:TURF TALK
TRAX-A-MILLION
ROBLO:DROOP-E
HAJI:MAC MALL
PROJECT BORN
E-40:TECH N9NE
KEAK DA SNEAK

MAC DRE
FIRE & RAIN

$3.95US $5.95CAN

BEEDA WEEDA:JOHNNY CASH:AMPLIVE:COOLNUTZ
REDMAN:AWAX:THE PACK:YOUNG BUCK:BIG RICH

MIKE JONES:50 CENT:HUSTLAMADE BUGZ:THE JACKA:LIL JON & THE EASTSIDE BOYZ

MURDER DOG

SPECIAL REPORT:
MAC DRE & THIZZ NATION

PLUS:
LUDACRIS:UGK
DAVID BANNER
GAME:DIRTBAG
DSR:HUSALAH
MONEY WATERS
MANNIE FRESH
ROBLO:T-ROCK
TOCKA:RYDAH

MAC DRE
7/5/70 - 11/1/04

EVIL PIMP:MAC MALL:YOUNG JEEZY:FAT KILLAHZ
KING TERRA:PAUL WALL:BLOODRAW:CUBAN LINK

SNOOP DOGG:YOUNG JEEZY:~~ICE~~ CUBE:THE GAME:LIL WAYNE:MAC DRE

MURDER DOG

PLUS:
- E-40:LIL BOOSIE
- BAVGATE:8 BALL
- UGK:TECH N9NE
- MESSY MARV:T I
- RICK ROSS:PSD
- M.O.S:JUVENILE
- DJ TOOMP:BELO
- ICE T:TRAXSTER

MURDER DOG: BEST OF THE BEST
2006
2006 YEAR END SPECIAL EDITION

WHAT THIZZ IS
MAC MALL:TRIPPIN

US $2.95 CANADA $3.95

MISTAH FAB:DJ DRAMA:ESHAM:JURASSIC 5:GUCE
OUTKAST:DEM HOODSTARZ:AL KAPONE:SAN QUINN

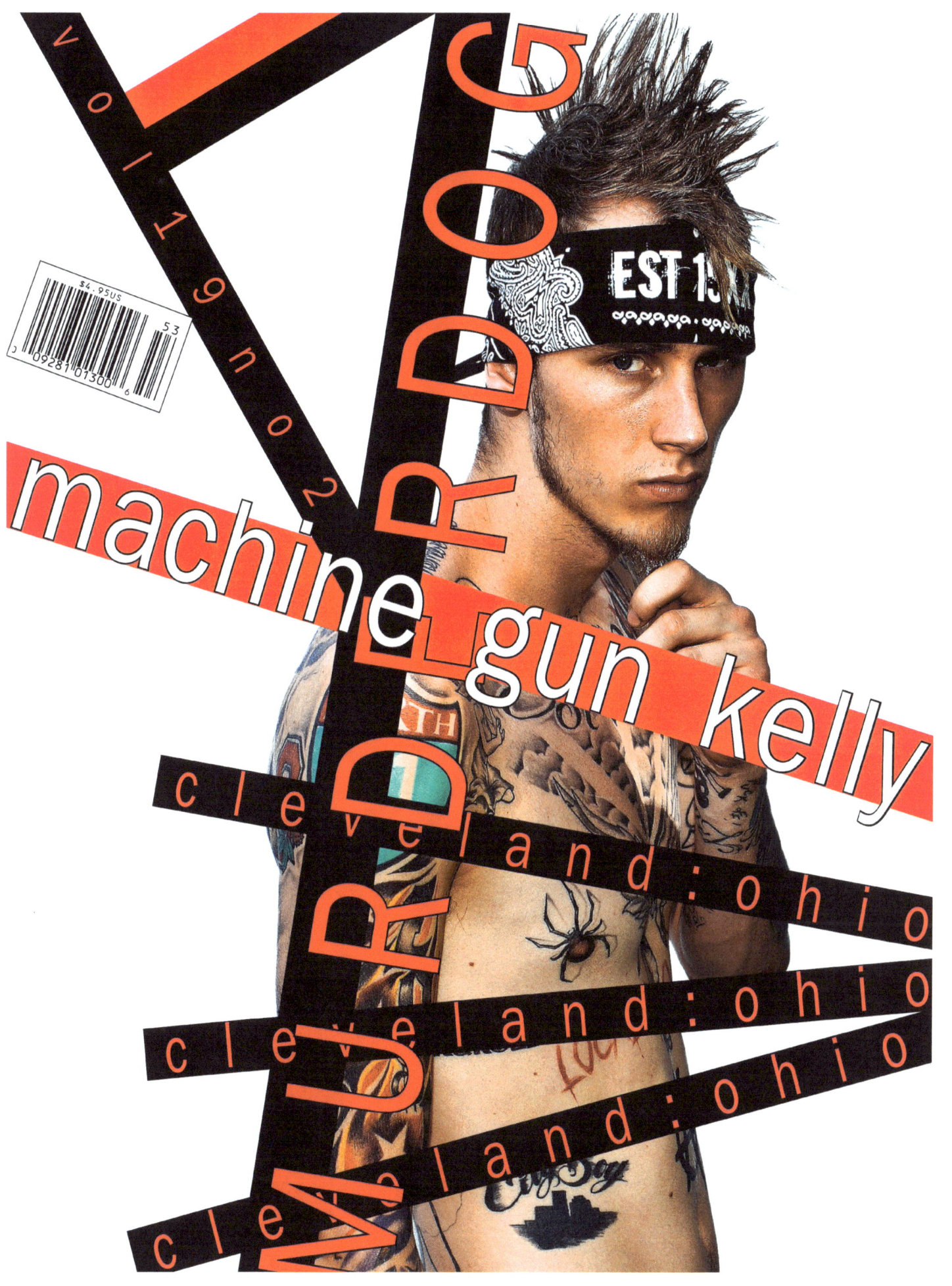

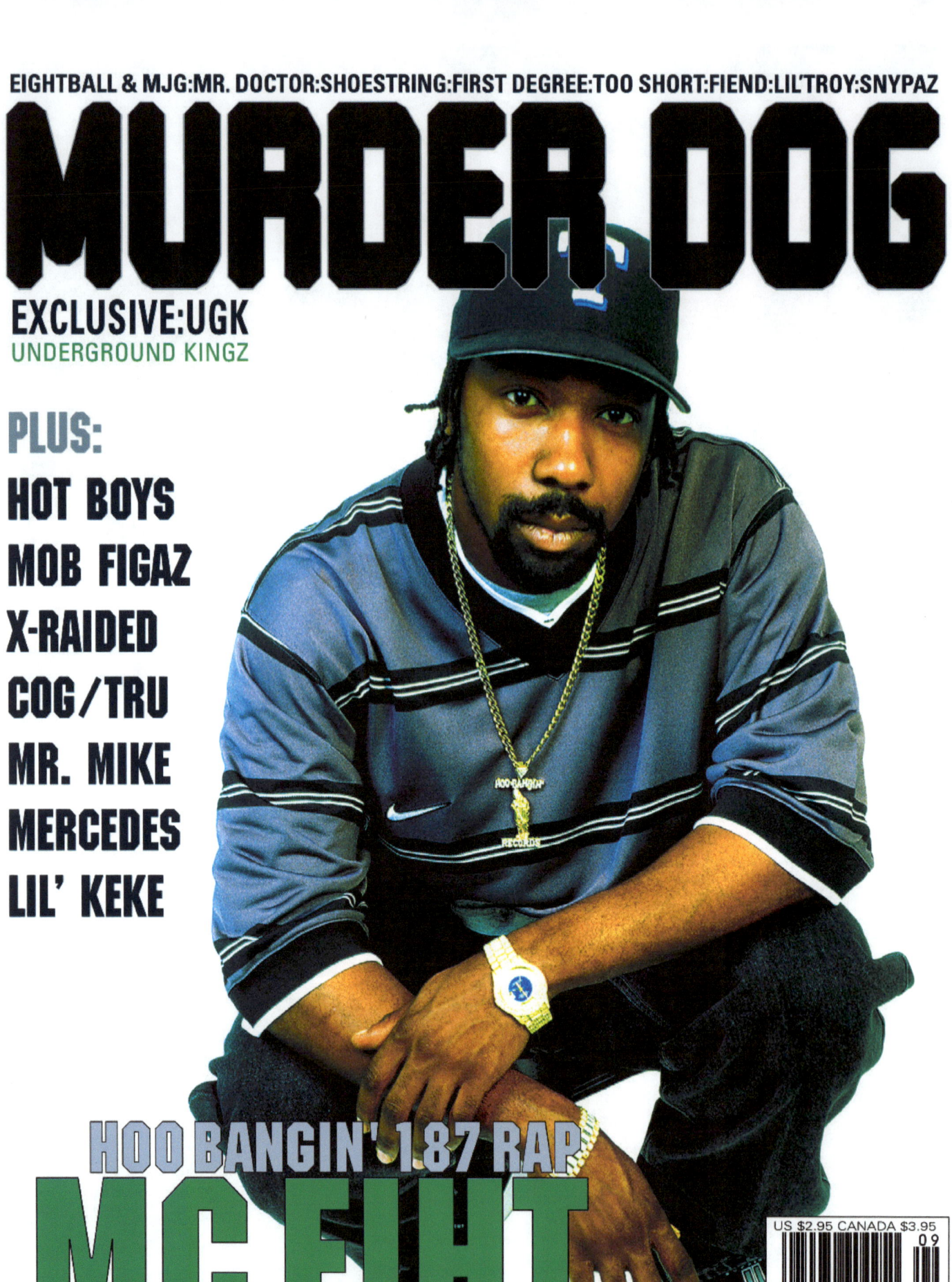

BONE CRUSHER:CASIDDY:KEAK... ...LJA SH... TWISTA:THUG LORDZ

MURDER DOG

PLUS:
- CHINGO BLING
- DAVID BANNER
- CYPRESS HILL
- INDIOTTA:TURK
- THUGGED OUT
- STREET LORDS
- BIG LURCH:BG

HYPNOTIC
MESSY MARV

US $3.95 CANADA $5.95

EASTSIDE CHEDDA BOYZ:C-MURDER:SAN QUINN
PASTOR TROY:COLO-RYDA:STAT QUO:GODXILLA

MAC DRE:CHAMILLIONAIRE:BONE THUGS-N-HARMONY:MIKE JONES:J-STALIN:HOODSTARZ

MURDER DOG

SPECIAL REPORT:
NEW BAY AREA PRODUCERS

PLUS:
PROPHET POSSE
ICE T:TURF TALK
TRAX-A-MILLION
ROBLO:DROOP-E
HAJI:MAC MALL
PROJECT BORN
E-40:TECH N9NE
KEAK DA SNEAK

MISTAH FAB
FASTEN YOUR SEAT BELT

BEEDA WEEDA:JOHNNY CASH:AMPLIVE:COOLNUTZ
REDMAN:AWAX:THE PACK:YOUNG BUCK:BIG RICH

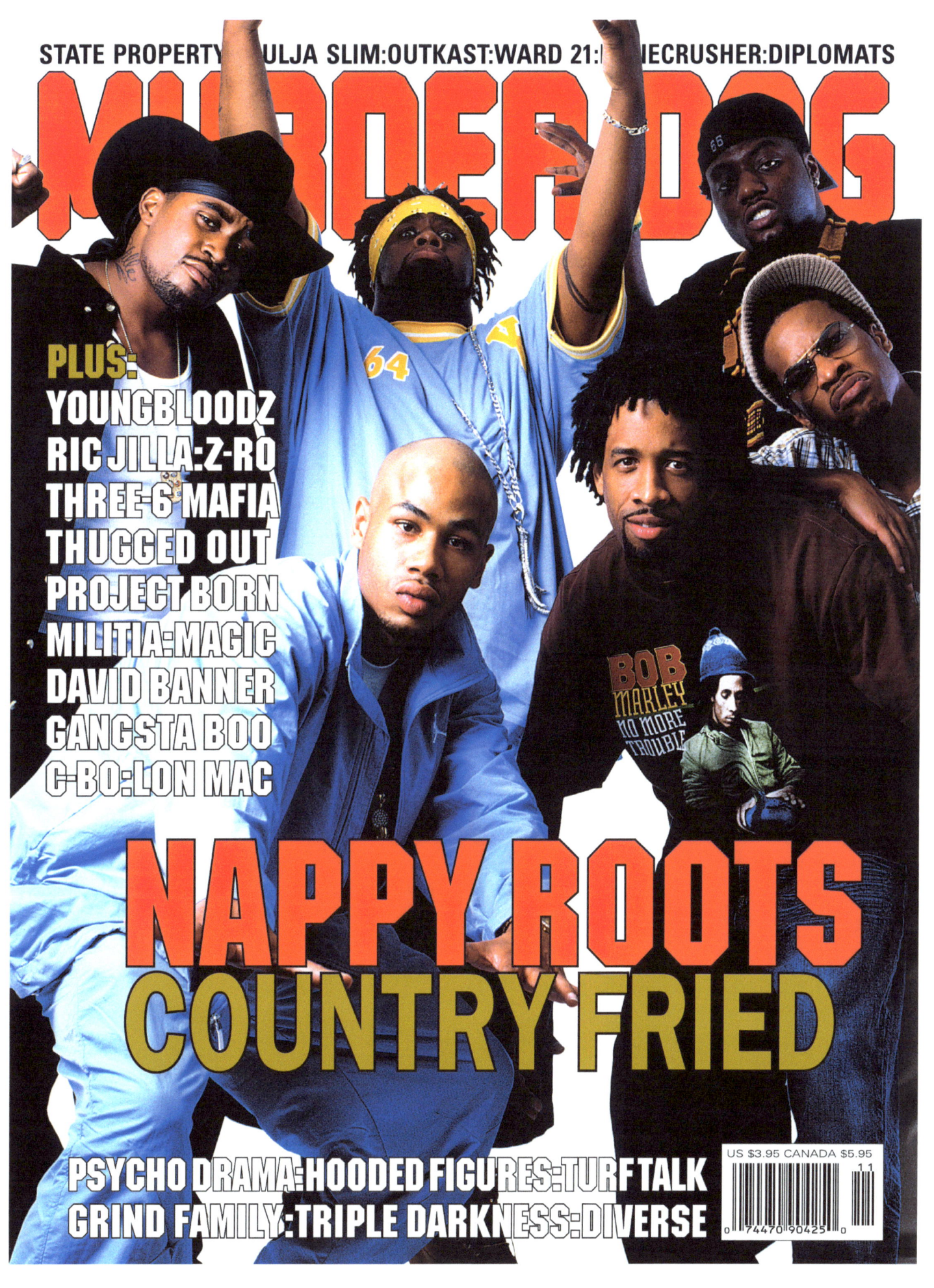

HOT BOYS:E-40:SHOESTRING:BIG POKEY:LIL' WAYNE:PROJECT PAT:MOBB DEEP:JUVENILE

MURDER DOG

**5TH WARD BOYZ
LIL'KEKE:B-LEGIT
X-RAIDED:T-MAC
KILLATAY:GUCE**

TOUCH & DIE
NATAS

GANGSTA BLAC:KACH.22:PSD:MAGIC:YUNGSTAR:TAYLOR BOYZ
ROGUE DOG VILLIANS:CJ MAC:KEAK DA SNEAK:1540:MAC DRE

STATE PROPERTY:SOULJA SLIM:WARD 21:BONECRUSHER:NAPPY ROOTS:DIPLOMATS

MURDER DOG

SPECIAL REPORT:
CHICAGO,IL/GARY,IN

PLUS:
YOUNGBLOODZ
RIC JILLA:Z-RO
THREE-6 MAFIA
THUGGED OUT
PROJECT BORN
MILITIA:MAGIC
DAVID BANNER
C-BO:LON MAC

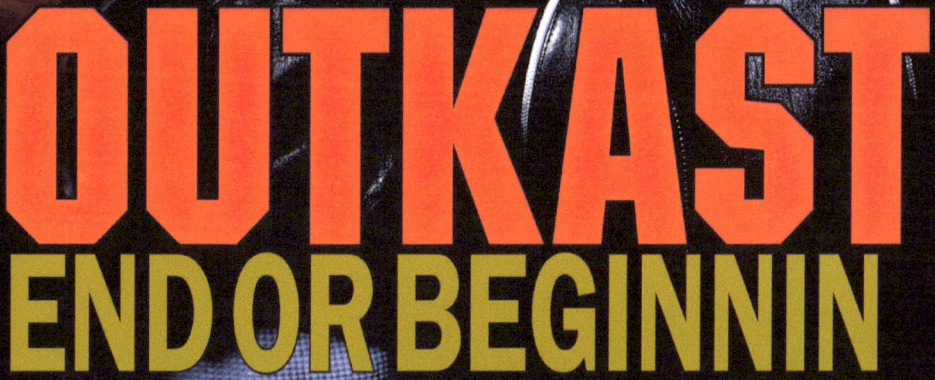

OUTKAST
END OR BEGINNIN

US $3.95 CANADA $5.95

PSYCHO DRAMA:HOODED FIGURES:TURF TALK
GRIND FAMILY:TRIPLE DARKNESS:DIVERSE

DAVID BANNER:YING YANG ... TONY YAYO:YOUNG JEEZY:WEBBIE

MURDER DOG

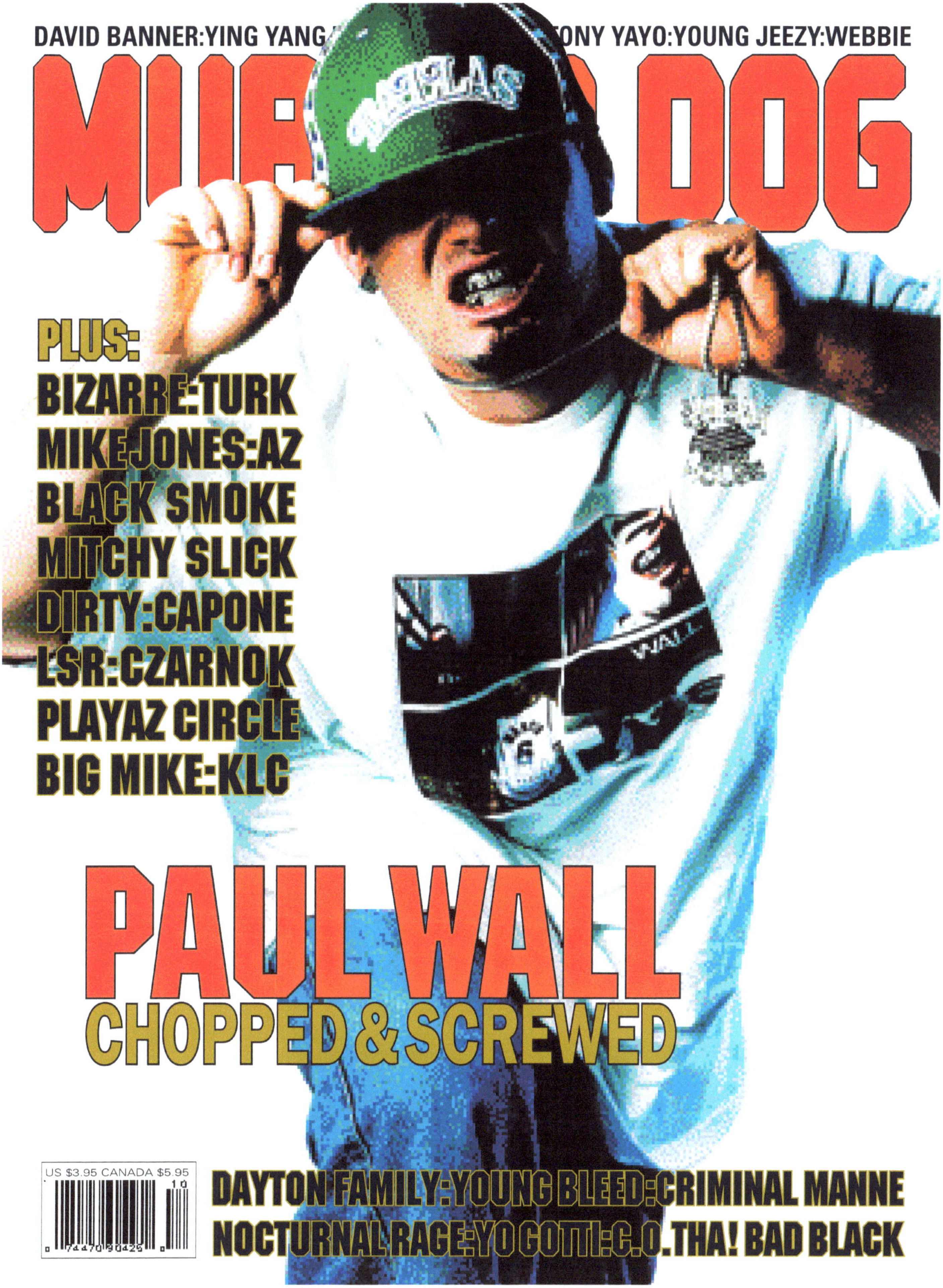

PLUS:
- BIZARRE:TURK
- MIKE JONES:AZ
- BLACK SMOKE
- MITCHY SLICK
- DIRTY:CAPONE
- LSR:CZARNOK
- PLAYAZ CIRCLE
- BIG MIKE:KLC

PAUL WALL
CHOPPED & SCREWED

US $3.95 CANADA $5.95

DAYTON FAMILY:YOUNG BLEED:CRIMINAL MANNE
NOCTURNAL RAGE:YO GOTTI:C. O. THA! BAD BLACK

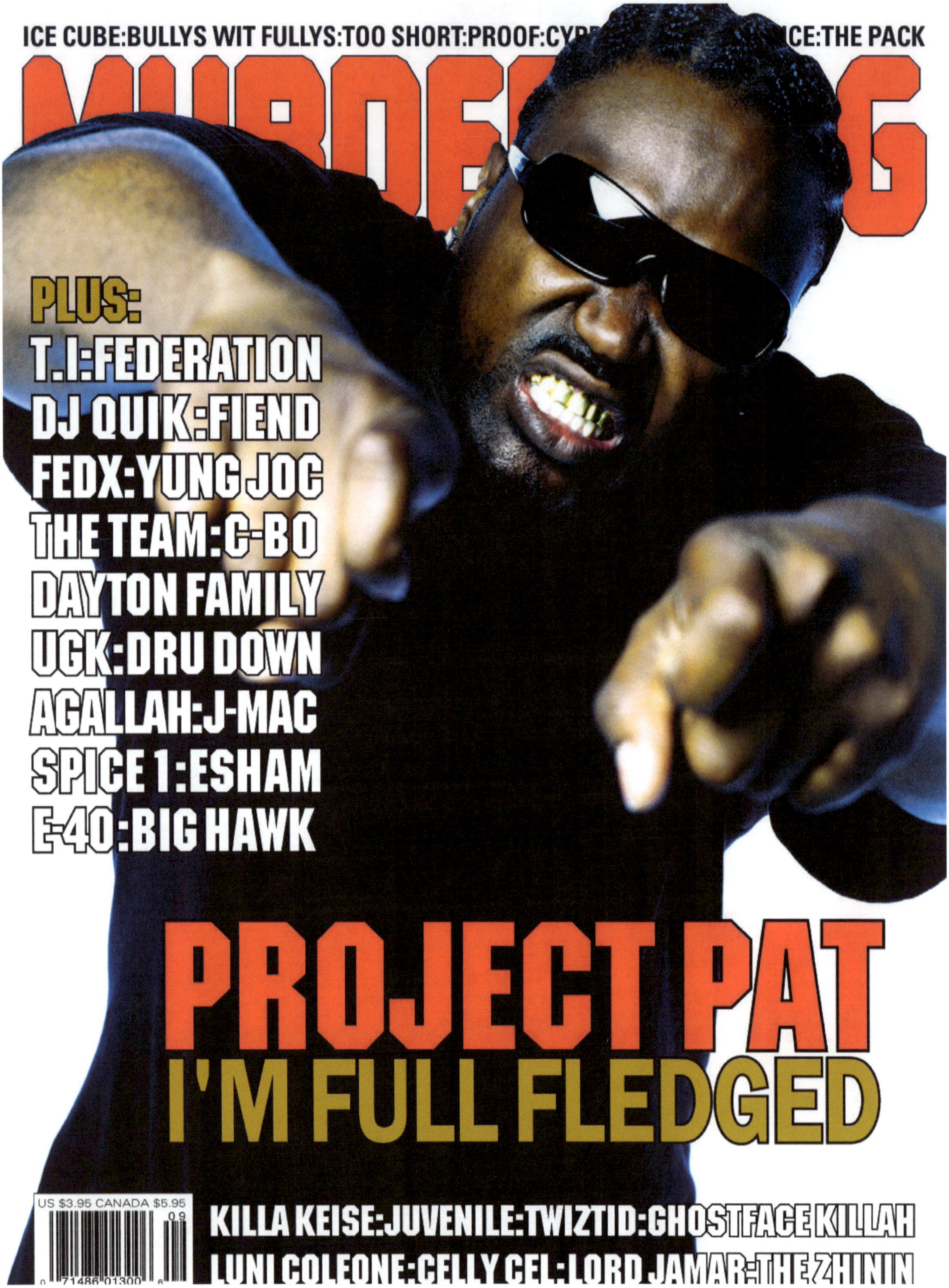

ICE CUBE:BULLYS WIT FULLYS:TOO SHORT:PROOF:CYPRESS:E-A-SKI:THE PACK

MURDER DOG

PLUS:
T.I:FEDERATION
DJ QUIK:FIEND
FEDX:YUNG JOC
THE TEAM:C-BO
DAYTON FAMILY
UGK:DRU DOWN
AGALLAH:J-MAC
SPICE 1:ESHAM
E-40:BIG HAWK

PROJECT PAT
I'M FULL FLEDGED

US $3.95 CANADA $5.95

KILLA KEISE:JUVENILE:TWIZTID:GHOSTFACE KILLAH
LUNI COLEONE:CELLY CEL:LORD JAMAR:THE ZHININ

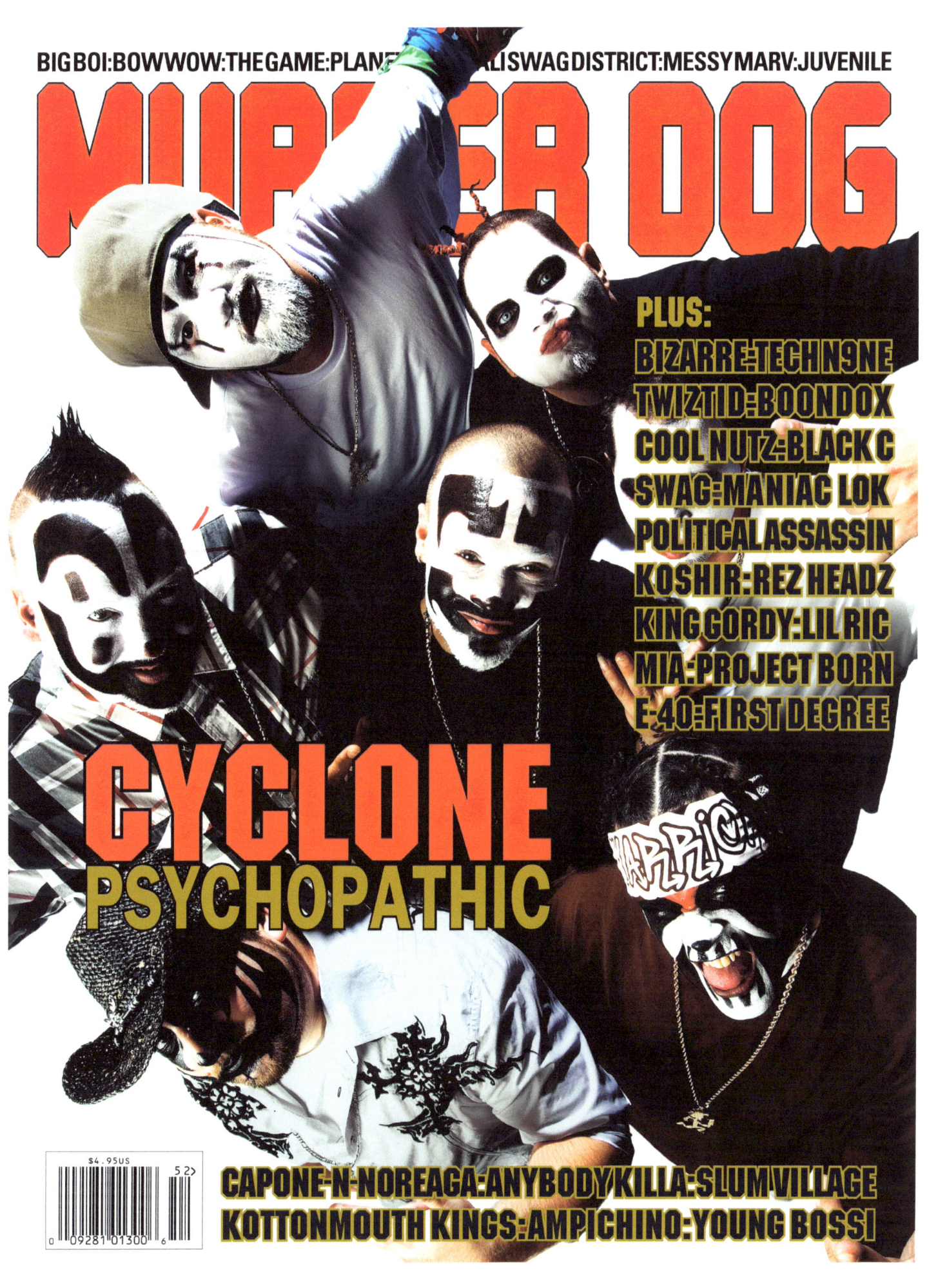

DR. DRE:AL KAPONE:PLAYA FLY:KURUPT:SERVIN THA WORLD CLICK:CHILEE POWDAH

MURDER DOG

SPECIAL FEATURE
DETROIT UNDERGROUND

PLUS:
COURT DOG
ICE T/KORN
BIG TYMERS
NATAS/E-40
COG/C-NOTE
HALF BREED

MURDER DOG READERS' POLL
BEST OF THE BEST
99
1999 YEAR END SPECIAL EDITION

RAEKWON
LIVE FROM NEW YORK

TWIZTID:INSANE CLOWN POSSE
PASTOR TROY:SKAMBINO MOB

LIL WAYNE:WEBBIE:SOULJA BOY:BIZZY BONE:SHA... ...WEST:BIRDMAN

MURDER DOG

PLUS:
FREEWAY:SEVEN
THE APHILLIATES
LITTLE BROTHER
EVOL:TOO SHORT
LORD INFAMOUS
PLIES:THE PACK
RYDAH J. KLYDE
PRODIGY:BUN B

FROM THE MURDER DOG ARCHIVES
PIMP C
EXCLUSIVE INTERVIEW & PHOTOS

RICKY ROSS

RICK ROSS
BIGGER & BETTER

$3.95US $5.95CAN

HURRICANE CHRIS:MITCHY SLICK:GUCCI MANE
MISTAH F.A.B:BERNER:TECH N9NE:PROJECT PAT

ICE CUBE:KOTTONMOUTH KINGS:GUCCI MANE:MUTT DOGG:BUSY SIGNAL:THE GAME

MURDER DOG

**SPECIAL FEATURE:
MALIDOMA SOME**

**PLUS:
DAZ:TECH N9NE
J-DIGGS:ESHAM
WILLIE THE KID
MAINO:J-STALIN
MJG:ACE HOOD
THREE 6 MAFIA
DEVIN:HAYSTAK
KUTT CALHOUN**

SAN QUINN
CITY 415 FEVA

**BEEDA WEEDA:LEP BOGUS BOYS:SUNNY VALENTINE
SKATTERMAN & SNUG BRIM:IMMORTAL SOLDIERZ**

FRANCHIZE BOYZ:D4L:GUCCI ROOKIE:E-40:KEAK DA SNEAK

MURDER DOG

PLUS:
PARIS:ICE CUBE
TOO SHORT:UGK
C-BO:MAC DRE
ICE T:RAS KASS
WU TANG CLAN
SPICE-1:ESHAM
SAN QUINN:BG
ICP:TECH N9NE

BEST OF THE BEST
804
MURDER DOG SPECIAL
INNOVATORS

SCARFACE
FIRST & LAST

US $3.95 CANADA $5.95

BUCK POWER:EAZY E:MESSY MARV:GETO BOYS
KILLA TAY:THREE 6 MAFIA:TRAP SQUAD:OUTKAST

MAC MALL:YOUNG JEEZY:CHAMILLI[ONAIRE:]DRE:LIL WAYNE

MURDER DOG

PLUS:
- E-40:LIL BOOSIE
- BAVGATE:8 BALL
- UGK:TECH N9NE
- MESSY MARV:T.I
- C-BO:JIM JONES
- RICK ROSS:PSD
- M.O.S:JUVENILE
- DJ TOOMP:BELO
- ICE T:TRAXSTER

SNOOP DOGG
THE BAD SLEEP WELL

MURDER DOG: BEST OF THE BEST

2006
2006 YEAR END SPECIAL EDITION

US $2.95 CANADA $3.95

MISTAH FAB:DJ DRAMA:ESHAM:JURASSIC 5:GUCE
OUTKAST:DEM HOODSTARZ:AL KAPONE:SAN QUINN

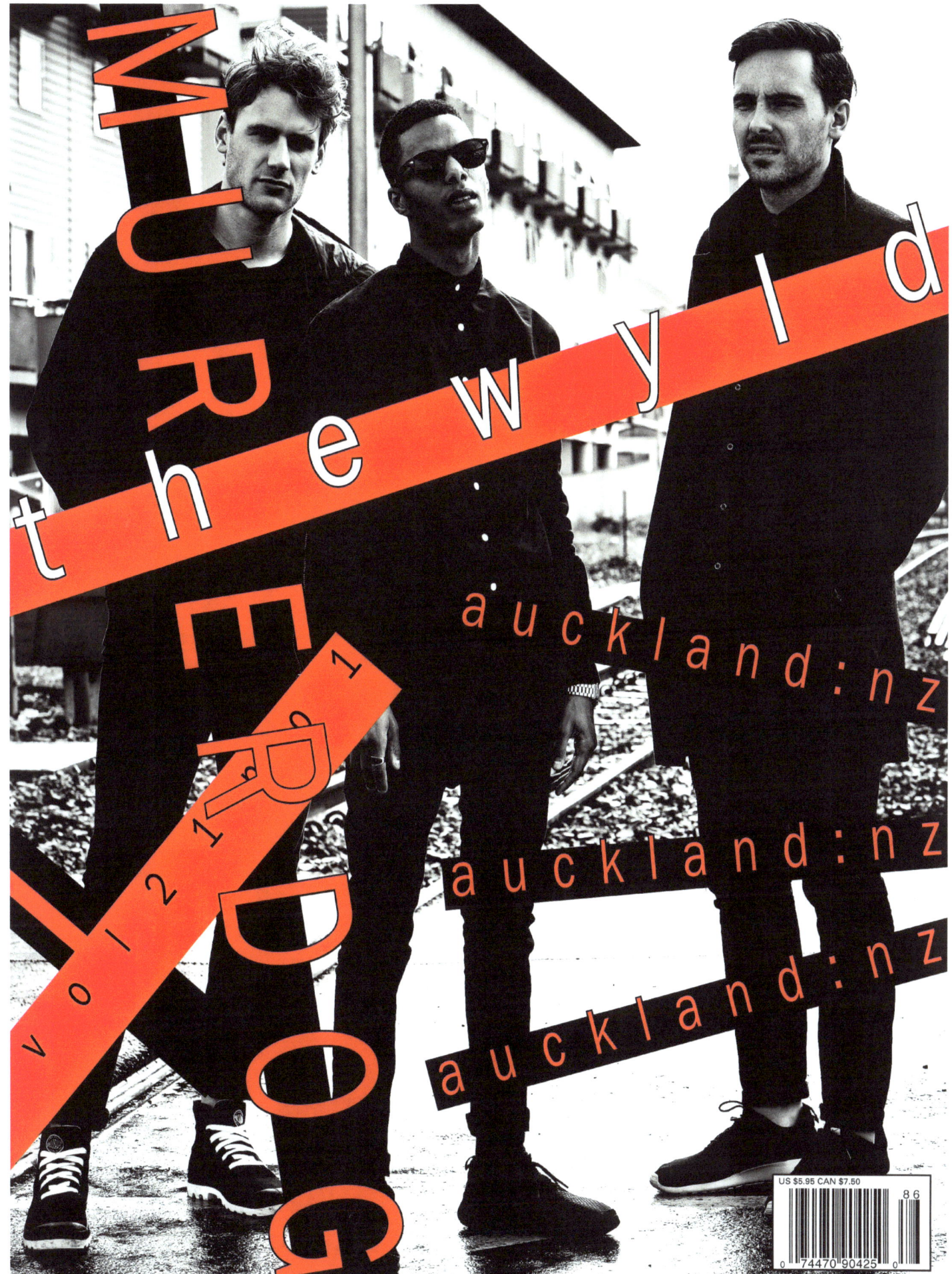

BONE CRUSHER:CUT THROAT COMITTY:LIL JO̶̶̶̶̶̶ MARV:KEAK DA SNEAK

MURDER DOG

PLUS:
CHINGO BLING
DAVID BANNER
CYPRESS HILL
INDIOTTA:TURK
THUGGED OUT
TWISTA:ESHAM
STREET LORDS
BIG LURCH:BG

SOULJA SLIM
9/9/77 - 11/26/03

US $3.95 CANADA $5.95

EASTSIDE CHEDDA BOYZ:C-MURDER:SAN QUINN
PASTOR TROY:COLO-RYDA:STAT QUO:GODXILLA

BLACK EYED PEAS:TRICK DADDY:LIL' O:DIRTY:EC ILLA:SOULS OF MISCHIEF:KRS ONE

MURDER DOG

SPECIAL REPORT:
WHO'S HOT IN THE BAY!

PLUS:
RBL POSSE
KAM:2PAC
DBA:ICONZ
MAC MALL
YUKMOUTH
JURASSIC 5
SAN QUINN

FUTURE OF HIP HOP
TALIB KWELI

SKINNY PIMP:MESSY MARV:HI-TEK:BIG PUN
DILATED PEOPLES:TOMMY WRIGHT III:SKEE 64

MURDER DOG

murderdogcollectorsissue

MURDER DOG COLLECTOR'S ISSUE

tech n9ne

murder

> Muthafuckas is like, "You about to send Eminem your vocals? He gonna outdo you." I'm like, I do me! How's somebody gonna outdo me? He's gonna do him, I'm gonna do me.

he is here, see for yourself

tech n9ne

$4.95US

X-RAIDED : JAY ROCK : GAME : YOUNG JEEZY : KRIZZ KALIKO
TECH N9NE : LIL WAYNE : YELAWOLF : WAKA FLOCKA FLAME

SAIGON:KANYE WEST:DIZZEE RASCAL:MASTER P:MIDWESTSIDERS:KEAK DA SNEAK

MURDER DOG

SPECIAL REPORT:
KANSAS CITY:PHILADELPHIA

PLUS:
SPICE 1:TURK
SURVIVALIST
MC EIHT:GUCE
THUGGED OUT
SKINNY PIMP
LLOYD BANKS
Z-RO:FINESSE

TECH N9NE
KANSAS CITY:THAT IS THAT

US $3.95 CANADA $5.95

ELEMENTAL LAW:MIKE JONES:BYRD2BANKS
PAPER DOLL:WESCROOK:HUSTLAMADE BUGZ

PROJECT PAT:ICE CUBE: THE PACK:JACKA:BULLYS WIT FULLYS

MURDER DOG

SPECIAL RE...
INNOVATORS OF...

PLUS:
T.I:FEDERATION
DJ QUIK:FIEND
FEDX:YUNG JOC
THE TEAM:C-BO
DAYTON FAMILY
UGK:DRU DOWN
AGALLAH:J-MAC
SPICE 1:ESHAM
E-40:BIG HAWK

TOO SHORT
ON A DEEPER LEVEL

US $3.95 CANADA $5.95

KILLA KEISE:JUVENILE:TWIZTID:GHOSTFACE KILLAH
LUNI COLEONE:CELLY CEL:LORD JAMAR:THE ZHININ

UGK:JACKA:G... ...ESSY M... ...IM JONES:BUSTA RHYMES:LIL WAYNE

MURDER DOG

MURDER...
MC BREED...

MURDER DOG: BEST OF THE BEST
2008
2008 YEAR END SPECIAL EDITION

PLUS:
ZION I:SAVAGE
PROJECT BORN
STAT QUO:LATE
KEAK DA SNEAK
TECH N9NE:BG
DICE:DJ FRESH
D-LO:SLEEPY D
PARIS:X-CLAN

POWERFUL
TI:KEEPIN IT GROUNDED

$3.95 US $5.95 CAN

DOJA CLIK:12 GAUGE SHOTTIE:OJ DA JUICE MAN
EDDI PROJEX:SLIM THUG:ALFAMEGA:SHADY NATE

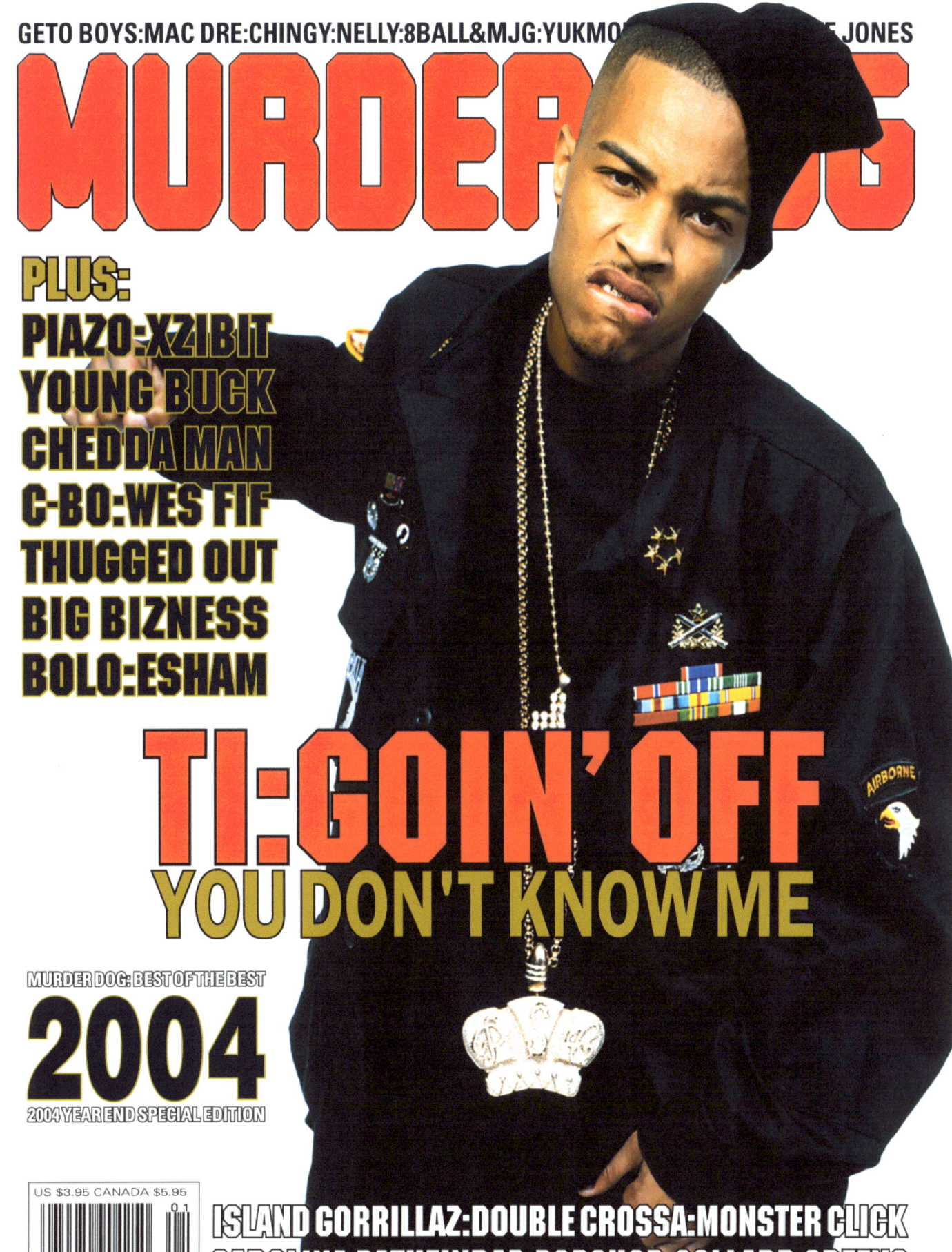

GETO BOYS:MAC DRE:CHINGY:NELLY:8BALL&MJG:YUKMO... ...E JONES

MURDER DOG

PLUS:
PIAZO:XZIBIT
YOUNG BUCK
CHEDDA MAN
C-BO:WES FIF
THUGGED OUT
BIG BIZNESS
BOLO:ESHAM

TI:GOIN' OFF
YOU DON'T KNOW ME

MURDER DOG: BEST OF THE BEST
2004
2004 YEAR END SPECIAL EDITION

US $3.95 CANADA $5.95

ISLAND GORRILLAZ:DOUBLE CROSSA:MONSTER CLICK
CAROLINA PATHFINDAZ:POPSHOP:COLLARD GREENS

RYE RYE:YUKMOUTH:DJ QUIK & KURUPT:HOOD:THE JACKA:GUCCI MANE

MURDER DOG

PLUS:
DIPLO:TECH N9NE
SANTIGOLD:JIBBS
ROD LEE:DRASTIC
SCOTTIE B:NOTTZ
BERNER:MAC DRE
D-LO:MATTY WACK
KING TUTT:B-CIDE
AX MURDER BOYZ

TOWN THIZZ
UPLIFTIN THE BAY

BEEDA WEEDA:SLEEPY D:BROTHA LYNCH HUNG
PHILTHY RICH:SONA:DENGUE FEVER:J-STALIN

U.S.D.A.:DROOP E:YUNG JOC:PASTOR TROY:PLANET ASIA:GRANDADDY SOUF:MUTT DOGG

MURDER DOG

SPECIAL REPORT:
MONTGOMERY, ALABAMA

PLUS:
- E-40:MAXXIMUM
- MAFIOSO:T-HUD
- LAROO:RAINMAN
- BOYZ-N-DA-HOOD
- JD WALKER:HAJI
- BLACK C:KALASO
- BEBOP:BIG TUCK
- YOUNG 'D' BOYZ

TURF TALK
HIGHSPEED WORLDWIDE

$3.95US $5.95CAN

BROTHA LYNCH HUNG:RAPPIN 4-TAY:FAT BASTARD
TUM TUM:DANNY TREJO:LIL CHAPPY:MR. DOGTOR

murderdogcollectorsissue

YOUNG MONEY

OG
murder

careless world
TYGA

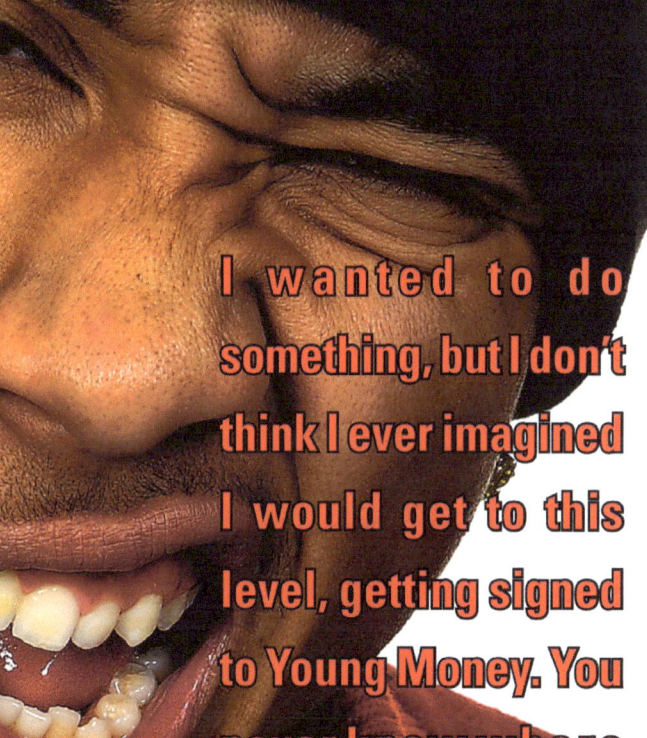

> I wanted to do something, but I don't think I ever imagined I would get to this level, getting signed to Young Money. You never know where it will take you.

$4.95US

X-RAIDED·BAD LUCC·B-CIDE·DON TRIP·T-NUTTY·PROZAK
TECH N9NE·PROBLEM·SPANK ROCK·MAYDAY·KILO CURT

LIL WAYNE:RICK ROSS:SHAWTY ... JA BOY:BIZZY BONE:BIRDMAN

MURDER DOG

PLUS:
FREEWAY:SEVEN
THE APHILLIATES
LITTLE BROTHER
EVOL:TOO SHORT
LORD INFAMOUS
PLIES:THE PACK
RYDAH J. KLYDE
PRODIGY:BUN B

FROM THE MURDER DOG ARCHIVES
PIMP C
EXCLUSIVE INTERVIEW & PHOTOS

WEBBIE
CHILLIN & SMOKIN

$3.95US $5.95CAN

HURRICANE CHRIS:MITCHY SLICK:GUCCI MANE
MISTAH F.A.B:BERNER:TECH N9NE:PROJECT PAT

G-UNIT:JUVENILE:DEAD PREZ:THREE 6 MAFIA:MEMPHIS BLEEK:NKMOUTH

MURDER DOG

PLUS:
- CELLSKI:PARIS
- E-40:SCARFACE
- YOUNGBLOODZ
- C-BO:MAC DRE
- JAY-Z:OUTKAST
- BG:OBIE TRICE

STATE OF EMERGENCY
WESTSIDE CONNECTION

MURDER DOG: BEST OF THE BEST
2003
2003 YEAR END SPECIAL EDITION

US $3.95 CANADA $5.95

KEAK DA SNEAK:STREET LORDZ:BOO YAA TRIBE
ECAY UNO:NEVA LEGAL:DUO LIVE:FAT KILLAHZ

RYE RYE:YUKMOUTH:ACE HOOD:DJ QUIK & KURUPT:TWIZTID:THE JACKA:GUCCI MANE

MURDER DOG

**MURDER DOG SPECIAL:
BALTIMORE:MD**

**PLUS:
DIPLO:TECH N9NE
SANTIGOLD:JIBBS
ROD LEE:DRASTIC
SCOTTIE B:NOTTZ
BERNER:MAC DRE
D-LO:MATTY WACK
KING TUTT:B-CIDE
AX MURDER BOYZ**

WALE
GREETINGS FROM NIGERIA

BEEDA WEEDA:SLEEPY D:BROTHA LYNCH HUNG
PHILTHY RICH:SONA:DENGUE FEVER:J-STALIN

MOBB DEEP:DIRTY:NAS:LA CHAT:RALLY :MURDER:JAYO FELONY:BUSTA RHYMES

MURDER DOG

SPECIAL REPORT:
PITTSBURGH, PA/MONTGOMERY, AL

- UGK:NEPTUNES
- CYPRESS HILL
- TOM SKEEMASK
- GANGSTA BLAC
- NATE DOG:JAY-Z
- SWISHAHOUSE
- BADDAZIS:AP.9
- GHETTO STARZ

MURDER DOG:BEST OF THE BEST
2001
2001 YEAR END SPECIAL EDITION

WARREN G
HEAVY WEIGHT

STRICT FLOW:MITCHY SLICK:8BALL:LONE CATALYSTS
RUFF CHEMISTRY:MOB TOWN HUSTLERS:BEN HATED

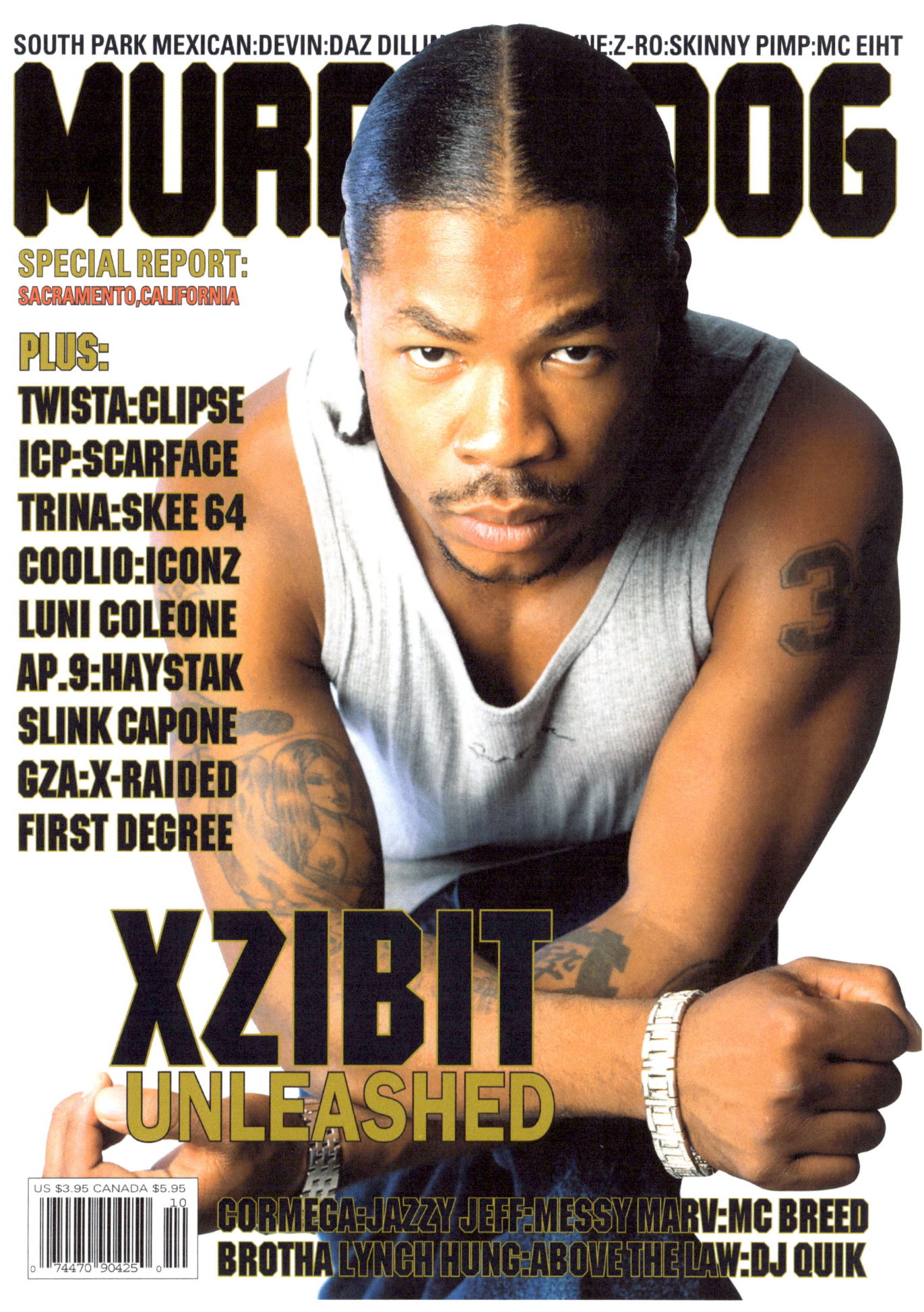

SNOOP DOGG:MAC MAL... ...GAME:LIL WAYNE:MAC DRE

MURDER DOG

PLUS:
E-40:LIL BOOSIE
BAVGATE:8 BALL
UGK:TECH N9NE
MESSY MARV:TI
RICK ROSS:PSD
M.O.S:JUVENILE
DJ TOOMP:BELO
ICE T:TRAXSTER

MURDER DOG: BEST OF THE BEST

2006
2006 YEAR END SPECIAL EDITION

YOUNG JEEZY
SIT BACK AND LAUGH

US $2.95 CANADA $3.95

MISTAH FAB:DJ DRAMA:ESHAM:JURASSIC 5:GUCE
OUTKAST:DEM HOODSTARZ:AL KAPONE:SAN QUINN

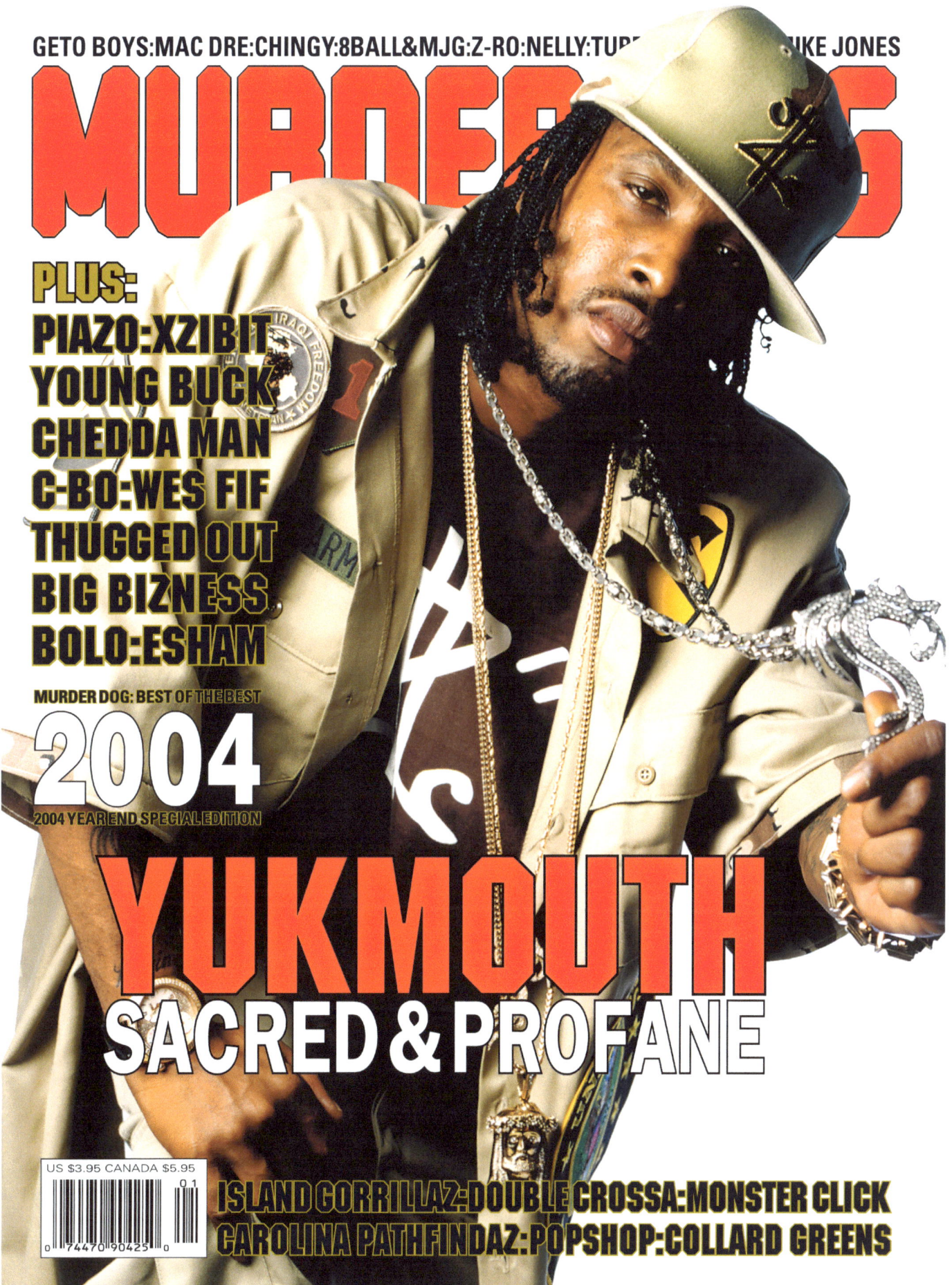

www.ingramcontent.com/pod-product-compliance
Lightning Source LLC
Chambersburg PA
CBHW041536220426
43663CB00002B/50